Word 2010: Advanced

Student Manual

MOS Edition

Word 2010: Advanced

Chief Executive Officer, Axzo Press:	Ken Wasnock
Series Designer and COO:	Adam A. Wilcox
Vice President, Operations:	Josh Pincus
Director of Publishing Systems Development:	Dan Quackenbush
Developmental Editor:	Chris Hale
Copyeditor:	Catherine Oliver
Keytester:	Cliff Coryea

For more information, go to www.logicaloperations.com

Trademarks

Disclaimer

Student Manual
ISBN 10: 1-4260-2168-2
ISBN 13: 978-1-4260-2168-8

Printed in the United States of America

1 2 3 4 5 GL 06 05 04 03

Contents

Introduction

After reading this introduction, you will know how to:

A Use ILT Series manuals in general.

B Use prerequisites, a target student description, course objectives, and a skills inventory to properly set your expectations for the course.

C Re-key this course after class.

Topic A: About the manual

ILT Series philosophy

Our manuals facilitate your learning by providing structured interaction with the software itself. While we provide text to explain difficult concepts, the hands-on activities are the focus of our courses. By paying close attention as your instructor leads you through these activities, you will learn the skills and concepts effectively.

We believe strongly in the instructor-led class. During class, focus on your instructor. Our manuals are designed and written to facilitate your interaction with your instructor, and not to call attention to manuals themselves.

We believe in the basic approach of setting expectations, delivering instruction, and providing summary and review afterwards. For this reason, lessons begin with objectives and end with summaries. We also provide overall course objectives and a course summary to provide both an introduction to and closure on the entire course.

Manual components

The manuals contain these major components:

- Table of contents
- Introduction
- Units
- Course summary
- Glossary
- Index

Each element is described below.

Table of contents

The table of contents acts as a learning roadmap.

Introduction

The introduction contains information about our training philosophy and our manual components, features, and conventions. It contains target student, prerequisite, objective, and setup information for the specific course.

Units

Units are the largest structural component of the course content. A unit begins with a title page that lists objectives for each major subdivision, or topic, within the unit. Within each topic, conceptual and explanatory information alternates with hands-on activities. Units conclude with a summary comprising one paragraph for each topic, and an independent practice activity that gives you an opportunity to practice the skills you've learned.

The conceptual information takes the form of text paragraphs, exhibits, lists, and tables. The activities are structured in two columns, one telling you what to do, the other providing explanations, descriptions, and graphics.

Course summary

This section provides a text summary of the entire course. It is useful for providing closure at the end of the course. The course summary also indicates the next course in this series, if there is one, and lists additional resources you might find useful as you continue to learn about the software.

Glossary

The glossary provides definitions for all of the key terms used in this course.

Index

The index at the end of this manual makes it easy for you to find information about a particular software component, feature, or concept.

Manual conventions

We've tried to keep the number of elements and the types of formatting to a minimum in the manuals. This aids in clarity and makes the manuals more classically elegant looking. But there are some conventions and icons you should know about.

Item	Description
Italic text	In conceptual text, indicates a new term or feature.
Bold text	In unit summaries, indicates a key term or concept. In an independent practice activity, indicates an explicit item that you select, choose, or type.
`Code font`	Indicates code or syntax.

`Longer strings of ►`
`code will look ►`
`like this.`
	In the hands-on activities, any code that's too long to fit on a single line is divided into segments by one or more continuation characters (►). This code should be entered as a continuous string of text.

Select **bold item**	In the left column of hands-on activities, bold sans-serif text indicates an explicit item that you select, choose, or type.
Keycaps like ↵ ENTER	Indicate a key on the keyboard you must press.

Hands-on activities

The hands-on activities are the most important parts of our manuals. They are divided into two primary columns. The "Here's how" column gives short instructions to you about what to do. The "Here's why" column provides explanations, graphics, and clarifications. Here's a sample:

Do it!

A-1: Creating a commission formula

Here's how	Here's why
1 Open Sales	This is an oversimplified sales compensation worksheet. It shows sales totals, commissions, and incentives for five sales reps.
2 Observe the contents of cell F4	 The commission rate formulas use the name "C_Rate" instead of a value for the commission rate.

For these activities, we have provided a collection of data files designed to help you learn each skill in a real-world business context. As you work through the activities, you will modify and update these files. Of course, you might make a mistake and therefore want to re-key the activity starting from scratch. To make it easy to start over, you will rename each data file at the end of the first activity in which the file is modified. Our convention for renaming files is to add the word "My" to the beginning of the file name. In the above activity, for example, a file called "Sales" is being used for the first time. At the end of this activity, you would save the file as "My sales," thus leaving the "Sales" file unchanged. If you make a mistake, you can start over using the original "Sales" file.

In some activities, however, it might not be practical to rename the data file. If you want to retry one of these activities, ask your instructor for a fresh copy of the original data file.

Topic B: Setting your expectations

Properly setting your expectations is essential to your success. This topic will help you do that by providing:

- Prerequisites for this course
- A description of the target student
- A list of the objectives for the course
- A skills assessment for the course

Course prerequisites

Students taking this course should be familiar with personal computers and the use of a keyboard and a mouse. Furthermore, this course assumes that students have completed the following courses or have equivalent experience:

- *Windows 7: Basic*, *Windows Vista: Basic*, or *Windows XP: Basic*
- *Word 2010: Basic*
- *Word 2010: Intermediate*

Target student

The target student for this course is an individual who wants to work more efficiently in Word 2010 and who wants to learn how to perform mail merges, create forms and macros, work efficiently in long documents, and customize Word.

MOS certification

This course is designed to help you pass the Microsoft Office Specialist (MOS) exam for Word 2010. For complete certification training, you should complete this course and all of the following:

- *Word 2010: Basic*
- *Word 2010: Intermediate*

Course objectives

These overall course objectives will give you an idea about what to expect from the course. It is also possible that they will help you see that this course is not the right one for you. If you think you either lack the prerequisite knowledge or already know most of the subject matter to be covered, you should let your instructor know that you think you are misplaced in the class.

Note: In addition to the general objectives listed below, specific Microsoft Office Specialist exam objectives are listed at the beginning of each topic (where applicable).

After completing this course, you will know how to:

- Create form letters, manage recipient lists, and print labels and envelopes.
- Insert content from other applications, and apply backgrounds to documents.
- Work with macros to automate tasks.
- Create and protect forms, and share and secure documents.
- Customize the Ribbon, the Quick Access toolbar, and keyboard shortcuts.
- Manage long documents by inserting tables of contents and figures, generating an index, and creating bookmarks and cross-references.
- Create and define an XML document.

Skills inventory

Use the following form to gauge your skill level entering the class. For each skill listed, rate your familiarity from 1 to 5, with five being the most familiar. *This is not a test.* Rather, it is intended to provide you with an idea of where you're starting from at the beginning of class. If you're wholly unfamiliar with all the skills, you might not be ready for the class. If you think you already understand all of the skills, you might need to move on to the next course in the series. In either case, you should let your instructor know as soon as possible.

Skill	**1**	**2**	**3**	**4**	**5**
Inserting and modifying mail-merge fields					
Specifying a starting document and a recipient list for a mail merge					
Customizing a form letter					
Creating a recipient list					
Merging recipient list data with a form letter					
Sorting records					
Filtering records					
Preparing and printing mailing labels					
Creating envelope documents from a recipient list					
Inserting content from other applications as linked or embedded objects in a Word document					
Modifying linked or embedded content from other applications					
Applying a background color to a document					
Applying fill effects to a document					
Inserting a watermark in a document					
Applying themes to a document					
Entering data in a form					
Adding field labels and content controls to a form					
Protecting a form and removing protection					
Setting permissions for a form user					
Using the Compatibility Checker					
Using the Document Inspector					
Publishing a file as an XPS document					

Skill	1	2	3	4	5
Using digital signatures					
Recording macros to automate tasks					
Running macros					
Modifying macros					
Copying and deleting macros					
Adding tabs, groups, and commands to the Ribbon					
Rearranging tabs on the Ribbon					
Adding buttons to the Quick Access toolbar					
Resetting the Quick Access toolbar and the Ribbon					
Adding and resetting keyboard shortcuts					
Creating a master document					
Adding a cover page					
Generating and updating a table of contents					
Generating and updating a table of figures					
Creating a table of authorities					
Creating an index					
Creating a bibliography					
Creating footnotes					
Working with bookmarks					
Working with cross-references					
Adding frames to a Web page document					
Attaching an XML schema to a Word document					
Applying XML tags to content					
Modifying XML options					
Testing the schema validation					
Using XML transforms and style sheets					

Topic C: Re-keying the course

If you have the proper hardware and software, you can re-key this course after class. This section explains what you'll need in order to do so, and how to do it.

Hardware requirements

Your personal computer should have:

- A keyboard and a mouse
- A 1 GHz (or faster) processor
- At least 1GB of RAM
- At least 1.5GB of available hard drive space after operating system install
- A monitor with at least 1024 × 768 resolution

Software requirements

You will also need the following software:

- Microsoft Windows 7
- Microsoft Office 2010
- A printer driver

Network requirements

The following network components and connectivity are also required for re-keying this course:

- Internet access, for the following purposes:
  - Downloading the latest critical updates and service packs
  - Completing activities throughout the course

Setup instructions to re-key the course

Before you re-key the course, you will need to perform the following steps:

1 Install Windows 7 according to the software instructions, or use a computer on which Windows 7 is already installed.

2 Install Microsoft Office 2010 according to the software manufacturer's instructions.

3 If you have the data disc that came with this manual, locate the Student Data folder on it and copy it to your Windows desktop.

   If you don't have the data disc, you can download the Student Data files for the course:

   a Connect to http://downloads.logicaloperations.com.
   b Enter the course title or search by part to locate this course
   c Click the course title to display a list of available downloads.
      Note: Data Files are located under the Instructor Edition of the course.
   d Click the link(s) for downloading the Student Data files.
   e Create a folder named Student Data on the desktop of your computer.
   f Double-click the downloaded zip file(s) and drag the contents into the Student Data folder.

Unit 1

Using Mail Merge

Unit time: 60 minutes

Complete this unit, and you'll know how to:

A Use the Mailings tab to create form letters.

B Create a recipient list, sort records, and filter records.

C Create mailing-label and envelope documents by using a recipient list.

Topic A: Form letters

This topic covers the following Microsoft Office Specialist objectives for exam 77-881: Word 2010.

#	Objective
7.1	**Set up a mail merge**
	7.1.1 Perform a mail merge using the Mail Merge Wizard
	7.1.2 Perform a mail merge manually
	7.1.3 Use Auto Check for Errors
7.2	**Execute a mail merge**
	7.2.1 Preview and print a mail merge operation

This topic covers the following Microsoft Office Specialist objectives for exam 77-887: Word Expert 2010.

#	Objective
4.1	**Execute a mail merge**
	4.1.1 Merge rules
	4.1.2 Send personalized email messages to multiple recipients
4.2	**Create a mail merge by using other data sources**
	4.2.1 Use Microsoft Outlook tables as data sources for a mail merge operation
	4.2.2 Use Access tables as data sources for a mail merge operation
	4.2.3 Use Excel tables as data sources for a mail merge operation
	4.2.4 Use Word tables as data sources for a mail merge operation

The Mail Merge feature

Explanation

When you need to mail a form letter to multiple recipients, you can save time by using Word's Mail Merge feature to generate all of the letters from a single document. Most of the text in the letter will be identical for all recipients, but some specific elements—such as the recipient's name and address—will be different in each letter.

Inserting standard fields

Before you begin the mail merge process, you might want to insert several standard fields into your letter. A *field* is a placeholder for data that can change. For example, you can use a field to insert a date that is automatically updated.

To insert a field:

1 Click the Insert tab.
2 In the Text group, click Quick Parts and choose Field to open the Field dialog box, shown in Exhibit 1-1.
3 From the Categories list, select a category.
4 Under Field names, select the field you want to insert.
5 Under Field properties and Field options, specify any additional settings needed.
6 Click OK.

In the document, fields are shaded gray when they're selected. Each field has a *field code*, which is the underlying instruction that provides the necessary result.

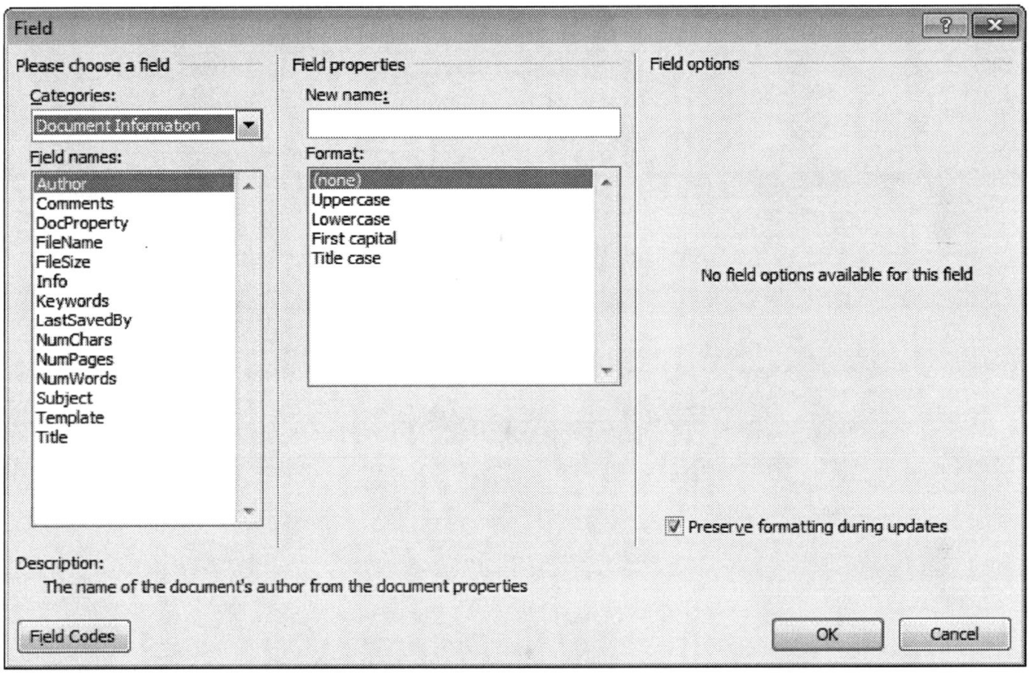

Exhibit 1-1: The Field dialog box

Do it!

A-1: Inserting a field

The files for this activity are in Student Data folder **Unit 1\Topic A**.

Here's how	Here's why
1 Start Microsoft Word	
Maximize the window	If necessary.
2 Open Letter	(From the current topic folder.) This will be the starting document for the mail merge.
Save the document as **My letter**	(In the current topic folder.) Before you begin the mail merge process, you'll insert and modify a few standard fields.
3 Scroll to view the name in the document's closing	The name "Chris Carr" appears at the end of the letter. You'll insert your name instead by using a field. First, you'll ensure that your name is specified as the author of this document.
4 Click the **File** tab	To display the document's standard properties. (On the File tab, the Info option is selected by default.)
Under Properties, right-click the **Author** box and choose **Edit Property**	
5 In the "Enter names or e-mail addresses" box, type your name	
Click **OK**	
Click the **Home** tab	To return to the letter.
6 Select **Chris Carr**	You'll insert the Author field to replace the selected text with your own name.
7 Click the **Insert** tab	
8 In the Text group, click **Quick Parts** and choose **Field...**	To open the Field dialog box.
9 From the Categories list, select **Document Information**	To display the Document Information fields.
Under Field names, verify that **Author** is selected	
Click **OK**	To insert your name as the document author.
10 Update the document	Click the Save button on the Quick Access toolbar.

Modifying fields

Explanation

After inserting a field, you can modify it by right-clicking it and choosing Edit Field to open the Field dialog box. The options in the Field dialog box will reflect the type of field you right-clicked. Specify the changes you want and click OK. If you change the data on which a field is based, you can update the field by right-clicking it and choosing Update Field.

Do it!

A-2: Modifying a date field

Here's how	Here's why
1 View the date at the top of the letter	The date was inserted as a field that always displays the current date. You'll modify the field to display a different date format.
2 Right-click the date and choose **Edit Field...**	To open the Field dialog box.
3 Under Date formats, select the sample date that uses the format **MMMM d, yyyy**, as shown	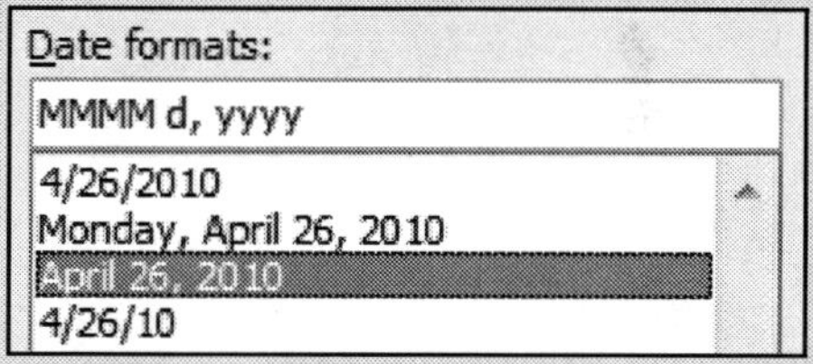 The date formats in the list will show the current date.
4 Click **OK**	The date uses the new format.
5 Update the document	

Steps in a mail merge

Explanation

To create a form letter, you'll use Word's Mail Merge feature. The mail merge options are located on the Mailings tab. Following is the basic procedure for performing a mail merge:

1. Create a starting document, which can be a letter, e-mail message, envelope, label, or directory.
2. Specify a list of recipients; this list should include the data that will change for each letter, such as name and address. You can create the data list in Word while you perform the mail merge, or you can use a list from another document or from your Outlook contacts.
3. Insert the data from the recipient list into the starting document. Each piece of data you insert is called a *merge field*. It appears as a placeholder representing data from the recipient list, as shown in Exhibit 1-2. The value in this field appears when you merge the starting document with the recipient list.
4. Merge the starting document with the recipient list. The merge fields are replaced with the data from the recipient list, as shown in Exhibit 1-3.

April 16, 2010

«AddressBlock»

«GreetingLine»

Because you are an important communicator in the food and restaurant industry in «City» and beyond, I invite you to take advantage of the enclosed press kit from Outlander Spices. Outlander Spices plays a unique and vital role in the food and restaurant industry, and I think you'll find that we provide information and perspectives you might not have encountered elsewhere.

Exhibit 1-2: A document containing merge fields

April 26, 2010

Mark Johnson
WLFF Radio
39 Elm Street
Portland, OR 97225

To Mark Johnson,

Because you are an important communicator in the food and restaurant industry in Portland and beyond, I invite you to take advantage of the enclosed press kit from Outlander Spices. Outlander Spices plays a unique and vital role in the food and restaurant industry, and I think you'll find that we provide information and perspectives you might not have encountered elsewhere.

Exhibit 1-3: A document after merging with a recipient list

Identifying a starting document and recipients

If you have a document containing a list of recipients, such as a Word table, an Excel spreadsheet, an Outlook table, or an Access table, you can specify that document as your recipient list. To specify a starting document and a recipient list document for a form letter:

1. Open or create the starting document that contains the letter text.
2. Click the Mailings tab, and in the Start Mail Merge group, click Start Mail Merge. From the menu that appears, choose Letters, as shown in Exhibit 1-4, to specify that the starting document is a letter.
3. In the Start Mail Merge group, click Select Recipients. From the menu that appears, choose Use Existing List, as shown in Exhibit 1-5. (To specify Outlook contacts as the source for your recipient list, click Select Recipients and choose Select from Outlook Contacts.)
4. In the Select Data Source dialog box, select the document you want to use, click Open, and click OK.

Exhibit 1-4: Specifying a form letter as the starting document for a mail merge

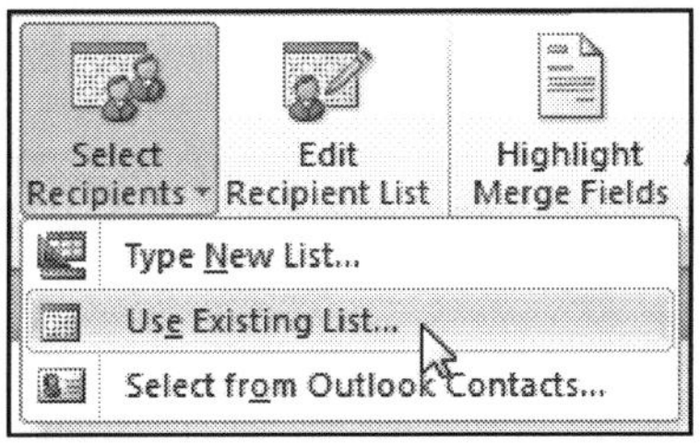

Exhibit 1-5: Specifying an existing document as the recipient list

The Mail Merge Wizard

You can use Word's Mail Merge Wizard to be guided through each step of the mail merge process. The wizard's steps and supporting information appear in the Mail Merge task pane. To start this wizard, click Start Mail Merge and choose Step by Step Mail Merge Wizard. The wizard is useful for those who aren't sure how to proceed with a mail merge. Usually, though, you can perform mail merges in fewer steps by using the tools on the Ribbon.

Do it!

A-3: Specifying a starting document and recipient list

The files for this activity are in Student Data folder **Unit 1\Topic A**.

Here's how	Here's why
1 Click the **Mailings** tab	
2 In the Start Mail Merge group, click **Start Mail Merge** and choose **Letters**	To specify that the starting document is a form letter.
3 In the Start Mail Merge group, click **Select Recipients** and choose **Use Existing List...**	To open the Select Data Source dialog box.
4 Navigate to the current topic folder	Student Data folder Unit 1\Topic A.
Select **Contacts**	You'll use this Excel file as the data source.
Click **Open**	The Select Table dialog box opens with the Employees worksheet selected.
Verify that **First row of data contains column headers** is checked	To indicate that the first row of data contains the headings for each column of data.
5 Click **OK**	You could click Edit Recipient List to open a dialog box displaying the recipient list data.
6 In the Start Mail Merge group, click **Edit Recipient List**	To open the Mail Merge Recipients dialog box. The list has seven recipients.
Click **OK**	To close the Mail Merge Recipients dialog box. You can now add merge fields, representing the recipient list data, to the letter.
7 Update the document	

Customizing form letters

Explanation

After you select a data source for the recipient list, you can customize your form letter by inserting fields from the data source. You can use the buttons in the Write & Insert Fields group, shown in Exhibit 1-6.

Exhibit 1-6: The Write & Insert Fields group on the Mailings tab

To customize a form letter:

1. In the form letter, place the insertion point where you want to insert the merge field.
2. In the Write & Insert Fields group, click Address Block to open the Insert Address Block dialog box, shown in Exhibit 1-7. You'll use this dialog box to insert the address merge fields.
3. From the "Insert recipient's name in this format" list, select a format for the merge field. By default, the company name and postal address are inserted along with the name field. You can clear these settings, if you prefer.
4. Click OK.
5. In the Write & Insert Fields group, click Greeting Line to open the Insert Greeting Line dialog box.
6. Select a greeting-line format and click OK.
7. In the Write & Insert fields group, click Insert Merge Field and choose the merge field you want to insert.

To make it easier to distinguish the merge fields from the other text in the document, you can click Highlight Merge Fields in the Write & Insert Fields group.

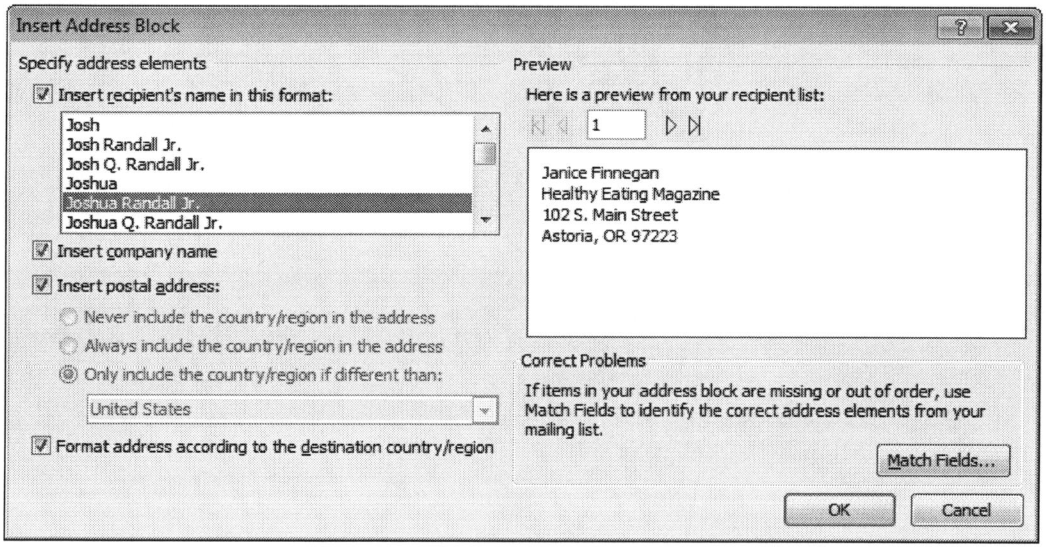

Exhibit 1-7: The Insert Address Block dialog box

Do it!

A-4: Customizing a form letter

Here's how	Here's why
1 Place the insertion point as shown	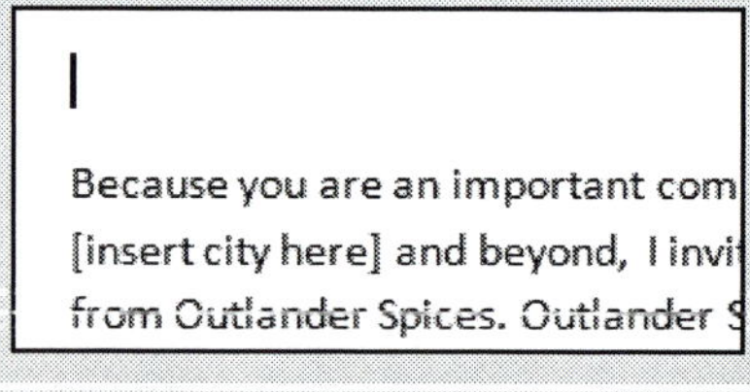
2 On the Mailings tab, in the Write & Insert Fields group, click **Address Block**	To open the Insert Address Block dialog box, shown in Exhibit 1-7. You can use this dialog box to insert one merge field that contains all of the address fields, such as street address, city, state, and ZIP code.
Click **OK**	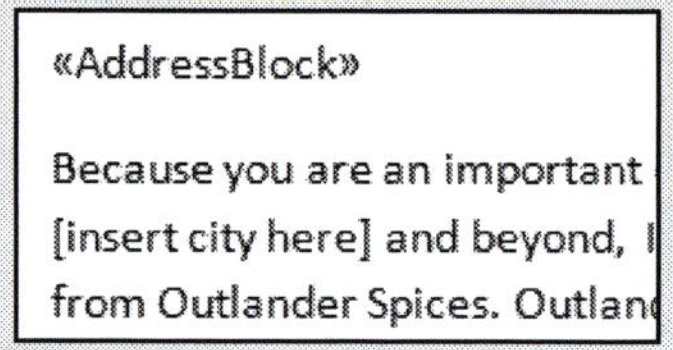 The AddressBlock field is inserted at the top of the document.
3 Press ENTER	To create a new line for the salutation.
4 In the Write & Insert Fields group, click **Greeting Line**	To open the Insert Greeting Line dialog box.
Under "Greeting line format," select **To**	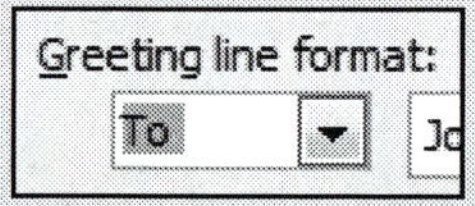
In the adjacent box, verify that **Joshua Randall Jr.** is selected	
5 Observe the Preview box	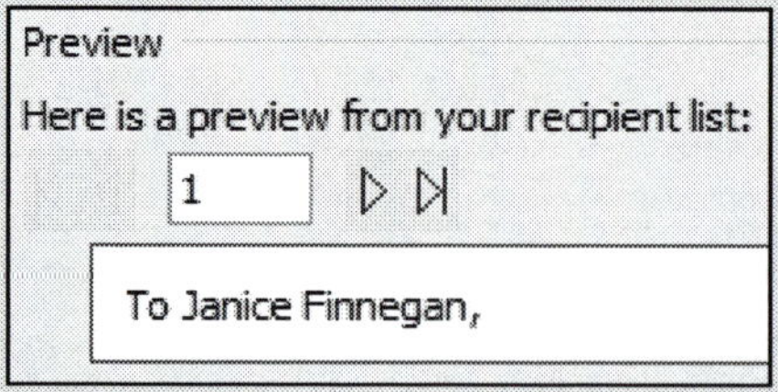 This box shows you how the greeting line will look in the document. The name that appears in this box is from your recipient list.
6 Click **OK**	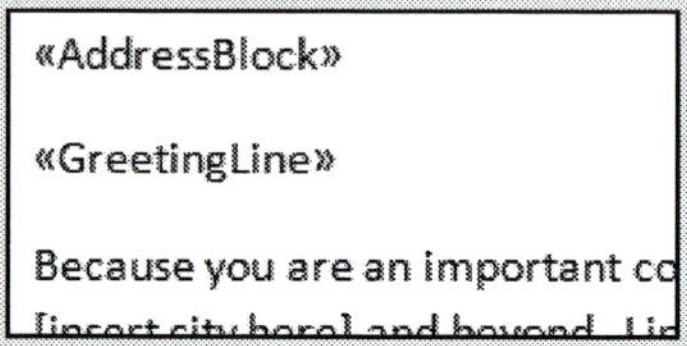 The GreetingLine field is inserted below AddressBlock in the document.

7	In the first sentence of the letter text, select **[insert city here]**	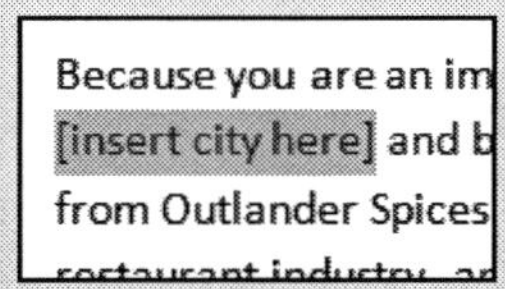 You'll insert the City field in this location, replacing the placeholder text.
	In the Write & Insert Fields group, click **Insert Merge Field**, as shown	 (Click the bottom part of the button.) To display a menu of possible fields.
	Choose **City**	To insert the City field in place of the selected text.
	If necessary, press SPACEBAR	To add a space after the City field.
8	In the Write & Insert Fields group, click **Highlight Merge Fields**	To add highlighting to the merge fields so that you can easily distinguish them from the letter text.
9	Observe the merge fields	Each merge field is now highlighted.
10	Update the document	

Merging recipient list data with form letters

Explanation

You can preview your form letters to see how they will look when printed. To do this, click Preview Results in the Preview Results group on the Mailings tab. The merge fields are replaced with the recipient information. To view each recipient's data, you can click the navigation buttons, shown in Exhibit 1-8.

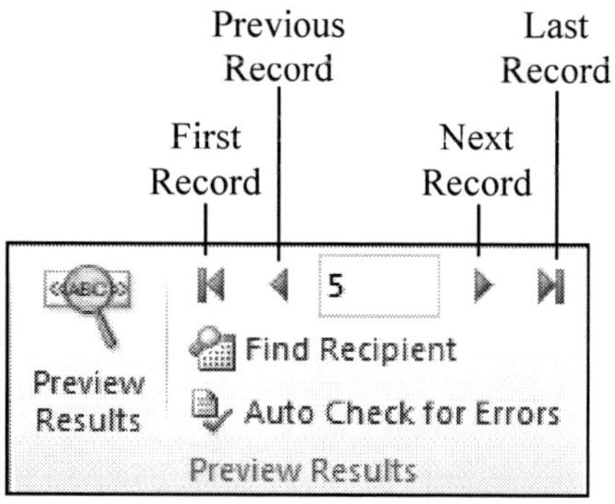

Exhibit 1-8: The Preview Results group on the Mailings tab

The following table explains the functions of the non-navigation buttons in the Preview Results group.

Button	Description
Preview Results	Displays the recipient list data in place of the merge fields.
Find Recipient	Used to search for and preview a specific record in a recipient list.
Auto Check for Errors	Used to specify how to handle errors that occur in a document file during a mail merge. Can also be used to simulate a mail merge to identify possible errors before the final merge is performed.

After finalizing the recipient data, you merge the data source with the form letter to generate a letter for each recipient. To do this, click Finish & Merge in the Finish group and choose Edit Individual Documents. All of the letters are generated within the current document, with a page break separating each letter. After you merge a data source, you can edit the letters individually or print them.

Sending personalized e-mail messages

You can use mail merge to send personalized e-mail messages to recipients. To do so, click Finish & Merge in the Finish group and choose Send E-mail Messages. In the Merge to E-mail dialog box, specify the To field (assuming that the data source contains e-mail addresses). To use this feature, you must have Outlook installed.

Using merge rules

You can specify rules that will affect how a mail merge is processed. In the Write & Insert Fields group on the Mailings tab, click Rules and select the desired rule.

Do it!

A-5: Merging recipient list data with a form letter

Here's how	Here's why
1 In the Preview Results group, click **Preview Results**	The AddressBlock merge field is replaced with the name and address of the first recipient. The GreetingLine merge field is replaced with the greeting line "To Janice Finnegan." Also, the City field in the first line of letter text is replaced with the first recipient's city.
2 Select the first three lines of address data	You'll remove the spacing below these lines.
Set the paragraph's Spacing After to **0** pt	Click the Page Layout tab. In the Paragraph group, under Spacing, enter 0 in the After box.
3 Click the **Mailings** tab	
4 In the Preview Results group, click 	To move to the next record in the data source. The information for Mark Johnson appears in the merge fields.
Continue until you've viewed all seven letters	The seventh letter is addressed to an employee at Outlander Spices. You'll create a rule to skip any record addressed to Outlander Spices.
5 In the Write & Insert Fields group, click **Rules** and choose **Skip Record If…**	To open a dialog box.
From the Field name list, select **Company**	
In the Compare to box, enter **Outlander Spices**	
Click **OK**	
6 In the Preview Results group, click 	To go to the sixth record. The rule won't work if the record containing the exception is selected.

7	In the Finish group, click **Finish & Merge** and choose **Edit Individual Documents…**	To complete the merge and create the form letters. The Merge to New Document dialog box appears.
	Verify that **All** is selected	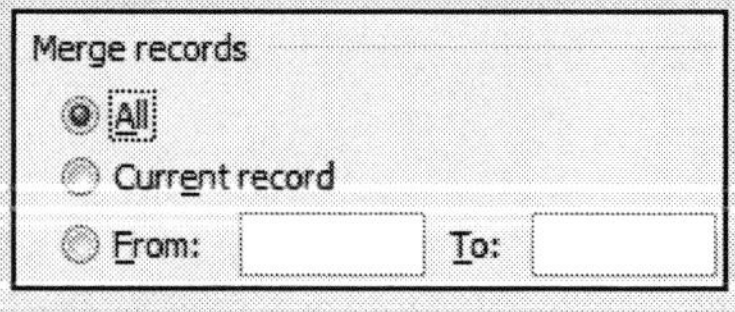
		In the Merge to New Document dialog box, you can select the records you want to merge. When All is selected, all of the letters will be merged in a new document, with each letter on a separate page.
	Click **OK**	A new document, Letters1, is created, with Janice Finnegan's letter on the first page.
	Scroll through the document	The names of other people in the data source appear. You can change individual letters and print each letter individually. Because of the "Skip Record If" rule you created, a letter addressed to Chris Carr does not appear.
8	Close the document	You don't need to save the changes in Letters1.
9	Update and close My letter	

Topic B: Data sources for the recipient list

This topic covers the following Microsoft Office Specialist objectives for exam 77-887: Word Expert 2010.

#	Objective
4.3	**Create labels and forms**
	4.3.1 Prepare data

Creating a recipient list

Explanation

When you're using a mail merge to create a form letter, you might already have the recipient list data in another document, such as an Excel spreadsheet or a Microsoft Word table. Having a data source ready is helpful, but there might be times when you need to create the recipient list during the mail merge. From the Select Recipients menu on the Ribbon, you can choose to type a new list. The New Address List dialog box provides some common fields for you to use. You can add or delete fields as needed.

To create a recipient list:

1. Specify the starting document.
2. In the Start Mail Merge group, click Select Recipients and choose Type New List to open the New Address List dialog box, shown in Exhibit 1-9.
3. Use the Customize Columns button to add or delete fields, if necessary.
4. In the dialog box, enter the data for each recipient.
5. Click OK and save the data source.

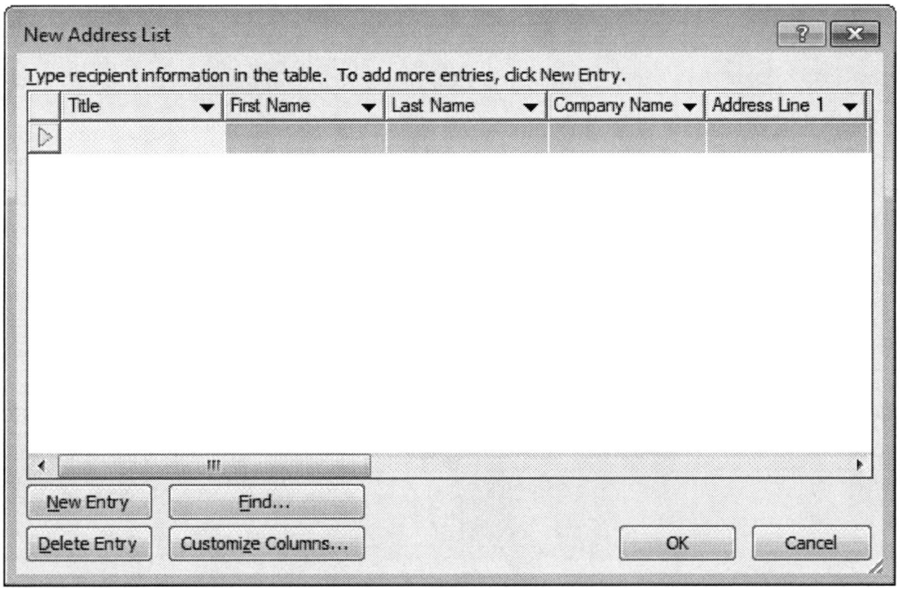

Exhibit 1-9: The New Address List dialog box

Do it!

B-1: Creating and using a recipient list

The files for this activity are in Student Data folder **Unit 1\Topic B**.

Here's how	Here's why
1 Open Letter2	You'll create a data source with the necessary fields and data.
Save the document as **My press kit letter**	
2 Click the **Mailings** tab	(If necessary.) You'll create a list of recipients.
In the Start Mail Merge group, click **Select Recipients** and choose **Type New List...**	To open the New Address List dialog box, shown in Exhibit 1-9.
Scroll to view all of the column headings	The column headings represent the fields that will hold the recipient data. The New Address List dialog box contains common fields for addresses, phone numbers, and e-mail addresses.
3 Click **Customize Columns**	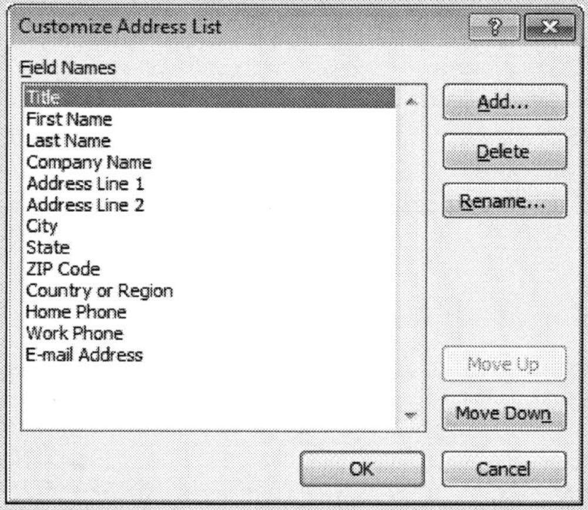 To open the Customize Address List dialog box, which you can use to add or delete fields.
Click **Delete**	To delete the selected Title field. You are prompted to confirm the deletion.
Click **Yes**	To confirm the deletion and close the message box.
4 In the Field Names list, select **Address Line 2**	You need only one address line.
Delete the field name	Click Delete and then click Yes to confirm the deletion.

5 Delete these fields:
Country or Region
Home Phone
Work Phone
E-mail Address

Select a field name in the Field Names list, click Delete, and click Yes.

If you needed any additional fields, you could click Add to add them now.

Click **OK**

To close the Customize Address List dialog box and return to the New Address List dialog box.

6 In the New Address List dialog box, enter the following data:
Rod
Yun
WBDR Radio
8201 Broadleaf Rd
Chicago
IL
60611

You can move from field to field by pressing Tab.

Type recipient information in the table. To add more entries, click New Entry.

	Company Name	Address Line 1	City	State	ZIP Code
	WBDR Radio	8201 Broadleaf Rd	Chicago	IL	60611

7 Click **New Entry**

To complete the first address-list entry and add a new row for the next entry.

8 Enter the following record data:
Tracy
McGarvey
Chicago Eateries Magazine
1191 Holmes Pkwy
Chicago
IL
60590

	Company Name	Address Line 1	City	State	ZIP Code
	WBDR Radio	8201 Broadleaf Rd	Chicago	IL	60611
	Chicago Eateries...	1191 Holmes Pkwy	Chicago	IL	60590

After entering the ZIP code, press TAB

To create another entry.

9 Enter the following record data:
Tanya
Poole
Classic Cooking Magazine
72 Lee St
Flint
MI
48532

10	Click **OK**	To close the New Address List dialog box and open the Save Address List dialog box.
11	Navigate to the current topic folder	Student Data folder Unit 1\Topic B. save as
	In the File name box, enter **My data source**	In the Save as type list, Microsoft Office Address Lists is selected. The data source will be saved as a Microsoft Office Address List.
	Click **Save**	To save the new address list. Now you'll designate this file as the recipient list.
12	Click **Select Recipients** and choose **Use Existing List...**	To open the Select Data Source dialog box.
	From the current topic folder, select **My data source**	You might need to navigate to the current topic folder.
	Click **Open**	To designate the selected file as the recipient list.
13	In your letter, insert the **AddressBlock** and **GreetingLine** fields, and then highlight the merge fields	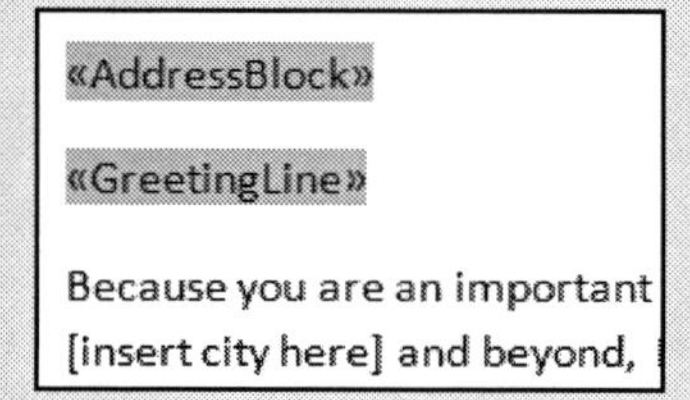 On the Mailings tab, click the Address Block and Greeting Line buttons and use the default settings. Click Highlight Merge Fields.
	In the body text, replace **[insert city here]** with the **City** field	Select "[insert city here]"; then click Insert Merge Field and choose City. Add a space after the field, if necessary.
14	Preview the letter	Click Preview Results.
	Remove the spacing below each of the first three lines of address data	Select the first three lines of address data. Click the Page Layout tab. In the Paragraph group, under Spacing, enter 0 in the After box.
15	Update the document	

The Mail Merge Recipients dialog box

Explanation

The Mail Merge Recipients dialog box, shown in Exhibit 1-10, displays all of the records in a data source. You can use this dialog box to sort and filter these records. To open the Mail Merge Recipients dialog box, click Edit Recipient List in the Start Mail Merge group.

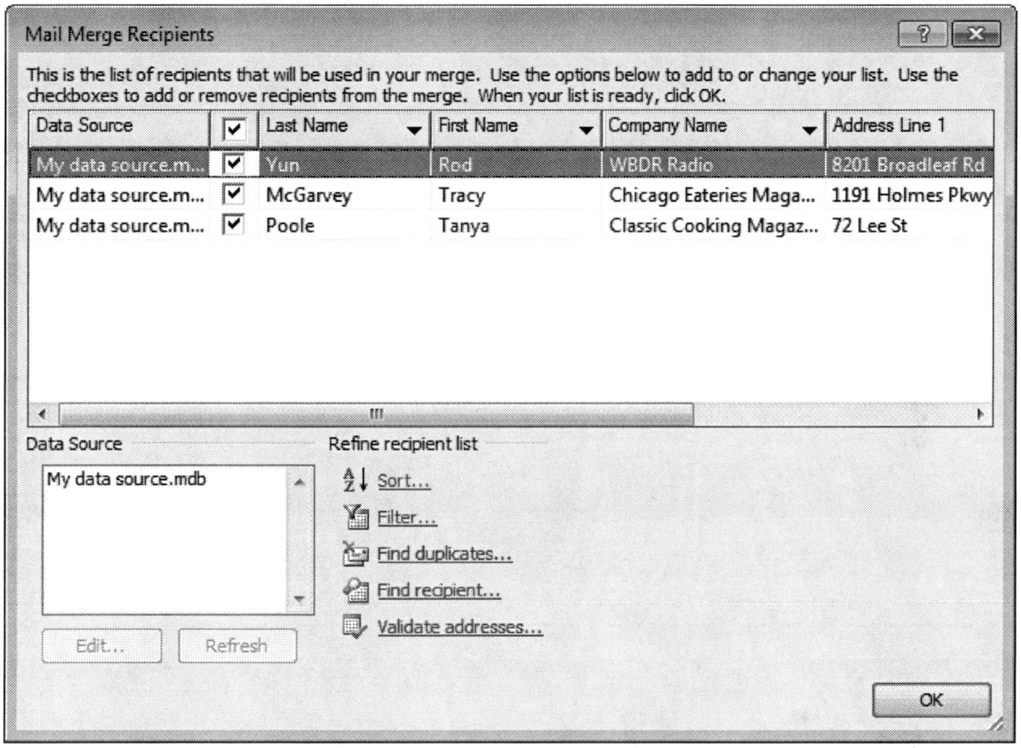

Exhibit 1-10: The Mail Merge Recipients dialog box

Sorting records

Before you print your form letters, you might want to sort the letters based on specific merge field data. For example, you might want to print the form letters in alphabetical order by last name. You can do this by sorting the records in the data source.

To sort records:

1. Open the Mail Merge Recipients dialog box.
2. Under Refine recipient list, click Sort to open the Filter and Sort dialog box, with the Sort Records tab active.
3. From the Sort by list, select the field by which you want to sort the recipients.
4. Select either Ascending or Descending.
5. Click OK to close the Filter and Sort dialog box.
6. Click OK to close the Mail Merge Recipients dialog box.

Do it!

B-2: Sorting records

Here's how	Here's why
1 In My press kit letter, observe the first record	The first record is Rod Yun.
Click the **Mailings** tab	If necessary.
2 Click 	(The Next Record button is in the Preview Results group on the Ribbon.) To move to the next record, which displays the information for Tracy McGarvey.
Move to the next record	The information for Tanya Poole appears.
Click 	(The First Record button.) To move back to the first record.
3 In the Start Mail Merge group, click **Edit Recipient List**	To open the Mail Merge Recipients dialog box, shown in Exhibit 1-10.
Under "Refine recipient list," click **Sort**	To open the Filter and Sort dialog box, with the Sort Records tab active.
4 From the Sort by list, select **Last Name**	The Ascending option is selected by default.
Click **OK**	To close the Filter and Sort dialog box. The records are sorted by last name in ascending order in the Mail Merge Recipients dialog box.
5 Click **OK**	To close the Mail Merge Recipients dialog box. The first record now displays the information for Tracy McGarvey.
Move to the second record	(Click the Next Record button.) The second record is Tanya Poole's.
6 Move to the first record	
7 Update the document	

Filtering records

Explanation

After creating form letters, you might decide to print only letters for a specific group of recipients. For example, you might want to send form letters to only those people who live in a particular city or who work in a particular department. To print only a subset of letters, you can filter out the other records.

To filter records in a data source:

1. Open the Mail Merge Recipients dialog box.
2. Click Filter to open the Filter and Sort dialog box, with the Filter Records tab active.
3. Specify the criteria for filtering the records, as shown in Exhibit 1-11.
4. Click OK twice to close the dialog boxes.

The difference between sorting and filtering is that when you sort, all records are displayed according to the sort condition. For example, if you sort by state in ascending order, then all records are listed, from Alabama to Wyoming. When you apply a filter, only those records that meet the filtering condition are displayed. For example, if you apply a filter for Illinois, then only those records with Illinois in the State field are displayed.

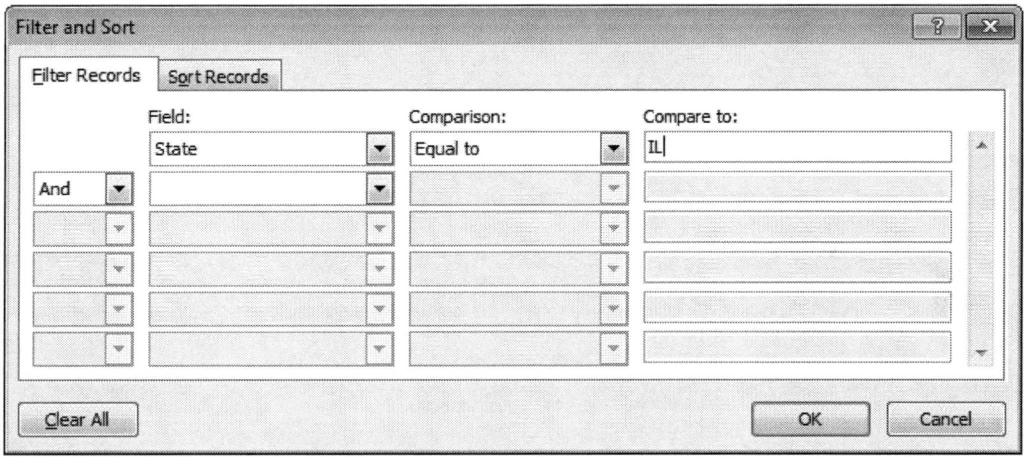

Exhibit 1-11: Filtering records

Do it!

B-3: Filtering records

Here's how	Here's why
1 Click **Edit Recipient List**	To open the Mail Merge Recipients dialog box. You'll create a filter to view only recipients from Illinois.
2 Under "Refine recipient list," click **Filter**	To open the Filter and Sort dialog box, with the Filter Records tab active.
3 From the Field list, select **State**	In the Comparison list, Equal to is selected.
4 In the Compare to box, enter **IL**	To specify a value for comparison, as shown in Exhibit 1-11.
Click **OK**	Only two records are shown in the Mail Merge Recipients dialog box.
5 Click **OK**	To close the Mail Merge Recipients dialog box.
6 View the two records	Use the Next Record button.
7 Update and close the document	

Topic C: Mailing labels and envelopes

This topic covers the following Microsoft Office Specialist objectives for exam 77-887: Word Expert 2010.

#	Objective
4.3	**Create labels and forms**
	4.3.2 Create mailing labels
	4.3.3 Create envelope forms
	4.3.4 Create label forms

Generating mailing labels

Explanation

In addition to creating form letters, you can use the Mail Merge feature to prepare mailing labels and envelopes. You do this by using the data in your recipient list. After performing the mail merge, you can print the results.

To use the Mail Merge feature to generate mailing labels:

1. Create a document and click the Mailings tab.
2. Click Start Mail Merge and choose Labels to open the Label Options dialog box.
3. Specify printer and label settings, as shown in Exhibit 1-12.
4. Click OK to create a sheet of blank labels.
5. Specify the recipient list.
6. In the label document, insert the necessary address fields in the first label.
7. Merge the data source with the label document.

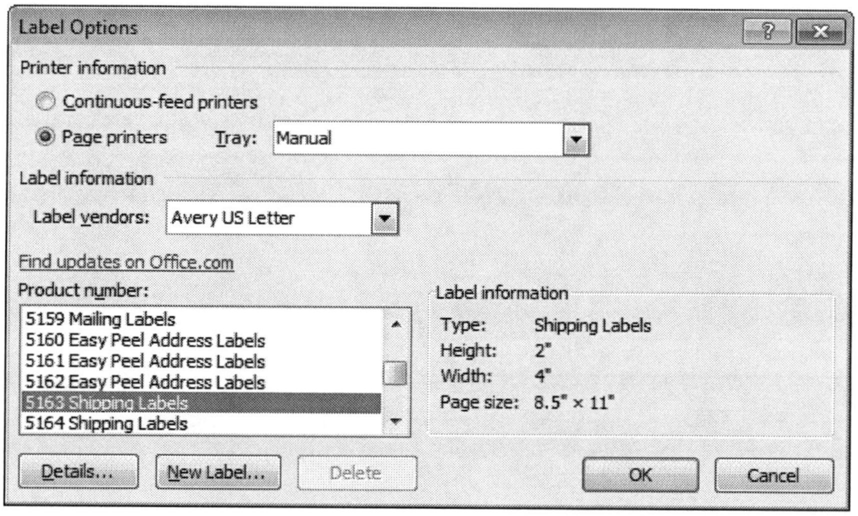

Exhibit 1-12: The Label Options dialog box

Do it!

C-1: Preparing mailing labels

The files for this activity are in Student Data folder **Unit 1\Topic C**.

Here's how	Here's why
1 Create a new blank document	
Save the document as **My labels**	In Student Data folder Unit 1\Topic C.
2 Click the **Mailings** tab	
Click **Start Mail Merge** and choose **Labels...**	To open the Label Options dialog box, which you'll use to specify printer and label settings.
In the Label vendors list, select **Avery US Letter**	To specify that you're using an Avery label.
From the Product number list, select **5163 Shipping Labels**	To specify the type of label and its dimensions. The Label information section of the dialog box displays the label type, dimensions, and page size.
Click **OK**	To close the Label Options dialog box and create a blank sheet of Avery address labels.
3 Specify **My data source** as the recipient list	(Click Select Recipients and choose Use Existing List. Select My data source and click Open.) The first label is blank, and the Next Record field appears in the other labels.
4 Insert the **AddressBlock** field	In the Write & Insert Fields group, click Address Block. Accept the default settings and click OK.
5 In the Write & Insert Fields group, click **Update Labels**	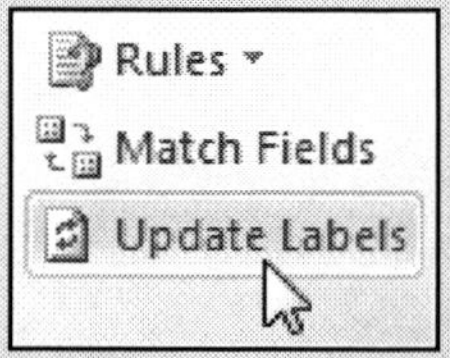 To insert the AddressBlock field in all of the labels.
6 Update the document	

Printing the labels

Explanation

After creating the mailing labels and inserting the merge fields, you're ready to complete the merge and print the labels. It's always a good idea to preview your labels before printing them.

To print the labels:

1. In the Finish group on the Mailings tab, click Finish & Merge and choose Print Documents. The Merge to Printer dialog box appears.
2. Under Print records, specify whether to print all of the records, the current record, or specific records. By default, All is selected.
3. Click OK to open the Print dialog box.
4. Change the print settings as needed, and click OK.

Do it!

C-2: Printing mailing labels

Here's how	Here's why
1 Click **Preview Results**	(In the Preview Results group on the Mailings tab.) The information in the data source records appears on the labels.
2 In the Finish group, click **Finish & Merge** and choose **Print Documents...**	To open the Merge to Printer dialog box. By default, All is selected.
3 Click **OK**	To open the Print dialog box.
4 Click **Cancel**	To close the Print dialog box without printing.
5 Update and close the document	

Using a list to generate envelope documents

Explanation

To use the Mail Merge feature to generate envelope documents:

1. Create a document and click the Mailings tab.
2. Click Start Mail Merge and choose Envelopes to open the Envelope Options dialog box.
3. Specify the envelope settings and click OK to create a blank envelope document.
4. Specify the recipient list.
5. Insert the necessary address fields in the envelope document.
6. Merge the data source with the label document.

Do it!

C-3: Creating envelope documents from a recipient list

Here's how	Here's why
1 Create a new blank document	If necessary.
2 Click the **Mailings** tab	
Click **Start Mail Merge** and choose **Envelopes...**	To open the Envelope Options dialog box.
Click **OK**	To accept the current envelope settings.
3 Click **Select Recipients** and choose **Use Existing List...**	
4 Specify **My data source** as the recipient list	You'll use this file as the data source.
5 Show paragraph marks	On the Home tab, in the Paragraph group, click the Show/Hide button.
Place the insertion point before the paragraph mark closest to the center of the envelope	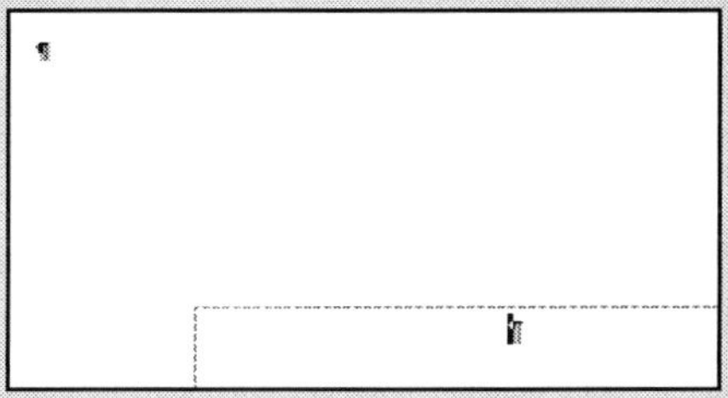 This is where the address will appear on the envelope.
Insert an **AddressBlock** field	Click Address Block and click OK.
6 Click **Preview Results**	(On the Mailings tab.) To see the envelopes as they will appear when printed.
Hide paragraph marks	On the Home tab, click the Show/Hide button.
7 Click the **Mailings** tab	
In the Preview Results group, click  twice	To preview the other records to be printed on envelopes.
8 Save the file as **My envelope list**	
Close the file	

Unit summary: Using Mail Merge

Topic A In this topic, you learned how to create **form letters** by using the Mail Merge feature. You added merge fields to a form letter and merged a recipient list with a form letter.

Topic B In this topic, you created a **recipient list**. You discussed the difference between **sorting** and **filtering** records. You also sorted and filtered records by using the Filter and Sort dialog box.

Topic C In this topic, you used the Mail Merge feature to prepare **mailing labels** and **envelopes** for printing. You prepared the mailing label and envelope documents, merged a data source with them, and printed the labels.

Independent practice activity

In this activity, you'll merge a starting document with a recipient list to create a form letter. You'll also generate mailing labels.

The files for this activity are in Student Data folder **Unit 1\Unit summary**.

1. Open Practice letter and save it as **My practice letter**.
2. Create a mail merge letter, using My practice letter as the starting document, and Practice contacts as the recipient list.
3. Insert the AddressBlock merge field, press Enter twice, and insert the GreetingLine merge field. Format the AddressBlock merge field to use 0 pt spacing after.
4. On the last line of the main paragraph, replace "[insert Division]" with the Division field.
5. Highlight the merge fields, preview the letter, and compare your screen to Exhibit 1-13.
6. Update and close My practice letter.
7. Create a new document and save it as **My practice labels**. You'll generate mailing labels for the form letter you just created.
8. Specify the document as a Labels starting document. In the Label Options dialog box, select Avery 5160 – Easy Peel Address labels.
9. Designate the Practice contacts file as the data source for the recipient list.
10. Insert the AddressBlock field, and update all of the labels in your document.
11. Preview your labels. If there's too much spacing between lines, select the first label, click the Page Layout tab, and set the Spacing After value to 0. Then return to the Mailings tab and click Update Labels. Compare your labels to those in Exhibit 1-14.
12. Update and close the document.

December 21, 2005

Anna Smith
101 Tread Road
Bend, OR 97701

Dear Anna Smith,

During the past few months, we've all been working very hard to make our company a success. Everybody's contributions are significant, but there are a few people who deserve special recognition for their outstanding performance and commitment in this busy time. I'm happy to tell you that the directors and I agree that you are our choice from the Marketing division to receive the enclosed gift certificate. You deserve it!

Thank you for your commitment to making our company a success!

Best regards,

Jake O'Connell, President
Outlander Spices

Exhibit 1-13: My practice letter after Step 5

Anna Smith 101 Tread Road Bend, OR 97701	Lisa Jones 90 Oak Street Portland, OR 97218	James Wilkins 1408 New Terry Street Oregon City, OR 97045
Don Allen 1074 4th Street Portland, OR 97220		

Exhibit 1-14: My practice labels after Step 11

Review questions

1 Which tab should you click to access the mail merge options?

A Home

B Insert

C Page Layout

D Mailings

2 What are the two primary components you need to perform a mail merge?

3 True or false? Before you can begin a mail merge, you must have the recipient list stored in an Excel spreadsheet.

4 What is an Address Block and how is it helpful in a mail merge?

5 Which button on the Ribbon can you click to display all of the records in the recipient list?

6 How can you specify that the current document is the starting document for mailing labels?

A Click Start Mail Merge and choose Labels.

B Click Start Mail Merge and choose Envelopes.

C Click Select Recipients and choose Use Existing List.

D Click Select Recipients and choose Type New List.

7 You've created a letter as the starting document for a mail merge. You want to use an existing Excel document as the source of the addresses for the mail merge. What should you do?

A Click Start Mail Merge and choose Directory.

B Click Start Mail Merge and choose Letters.

C Click Select Recipients and choose Use Existing List.

D Click Select Recipients and choose Type New List.

Unit 2

Objects and backgrounds

Unit time: 60 minutes

Complete this unit, and you'll know how to:

A Add content from other applications to a Word document by using Object Linking and Embedding.

B Customize a document's appearance by applying background colors, fill effects, watermarks, and themes.

Topic A: Inserting content from other applications

This topic covers the following Microsoft Office Specialist objectives for exam 77-887: Word Expert 2010.

#	Objective
2.2	**Create tables and charts**
	2.2.1 Insert tables by using Microsoft Excel data in tables
	2.2.3 Modify chart data
	2.2.4 Save a chart as a template
	2.2.5 Modify a chart layout

Working with objects

Explanation

You can insert content from other applications into Word and maintain the ability to edit the content in its original application so that it's updated in the Word document. To do this, you must use applications that support *Object Linking and Embedding* (OLE). When you insert content in this way, that content is referred to as an *object.*

You have several options for adding content as objects. You can insert a file or part of a file—such as an Excel worksheet—into your Word document. This file can be either linked to the source file or embedded as a standalone object. You can also insert a new object—such as a blank Excel worksheet—and then add your content.

Creating objects

To create a new object in a Word document:

1. In the document, place the insertion point where you want the object to appear.
2. Click the Insert tab.
3. Click Object to open the Object dialog box, shown in Exhibit 2-1.
4. In the Object type list, select the type of object you want to insert (for example, Microsoft Excel Worksheet). The items in the list will vary based on the software you have installed that supports OLE.
5. Click OK. An object appears in your document, displayed in the environment of the application you'll use to create the object. (If you insert an Excel Worksheet object, for example, a blank worksheet will appear, along with the Excel Ribbon.)
6. Add your content. (For example, enter your data into the worksheet.)
7. Click outside the object to return to the Word environment.

After creating an object, you can modify it in the application you used to create it. Just double-click the object and make your changes. Then click outside the object to return to the Word environment.

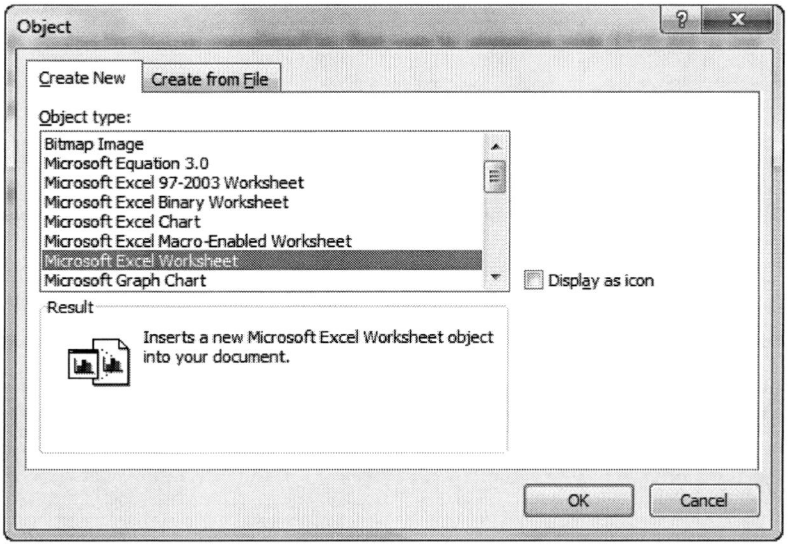

Exhibit 2-1: The Object dialog box

Do it!

A-1: Inserting an Excel worksheet

The files for this activity are in Student Data folder **Unit 2\Topic A**.

Here's how	Here's why
1 Open New objects	
Save the document as **My new objects**	(In the current topic folder.) You'll insert an Excel worksheet into this document to display numeric data with calculations.
2 Click below the document text	To place the insertion point below the text.
3 Click the **Insert** tab	
4 In the Text group, click **Object**	To open the Object dialog box.
5 In the Object type list, select **Microsoft Excel Worksheet**	As shown in Exhibit 2-1.
Click **OK**	A blank Excel worksheet appears in the Word document, and the Excel Ribbon and other controls appear in place of the Word tools. You can now add worksheet data, just as you would when working in Excel.
6 Click cell B1	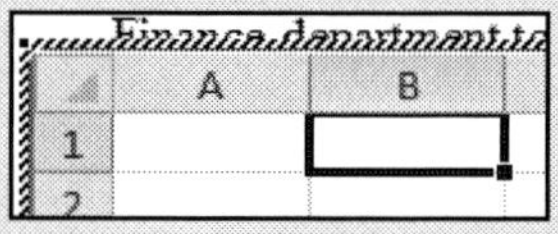 (Click in column B, row 1.) To activate that cell so you can enter data in it.
7 Type **Qtr 1**	To enter a column heading.
Press TAB	To select the cell to the right, which is cell C1.
8 Type **Qtr 2**	
Press ↓	To select cell C2, below the cell where you entered "Qtr 2."
9 Type **1750500**	To enter the sales estimate for the second quarter of next year.
Press SHIFT + TAB	To select cell B2.
10 Type **1575000**	
Press ↵ ENTER	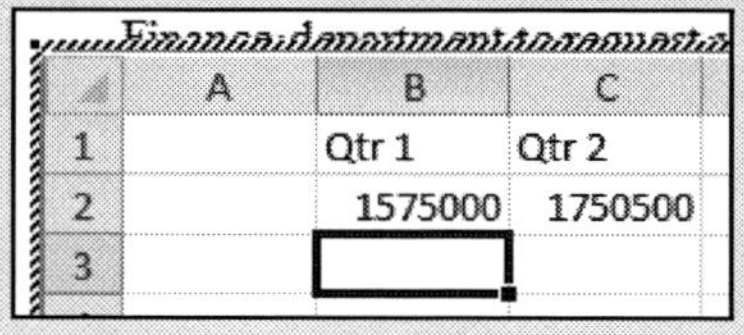

11	Click within the Word document text	To return to the Word environment.

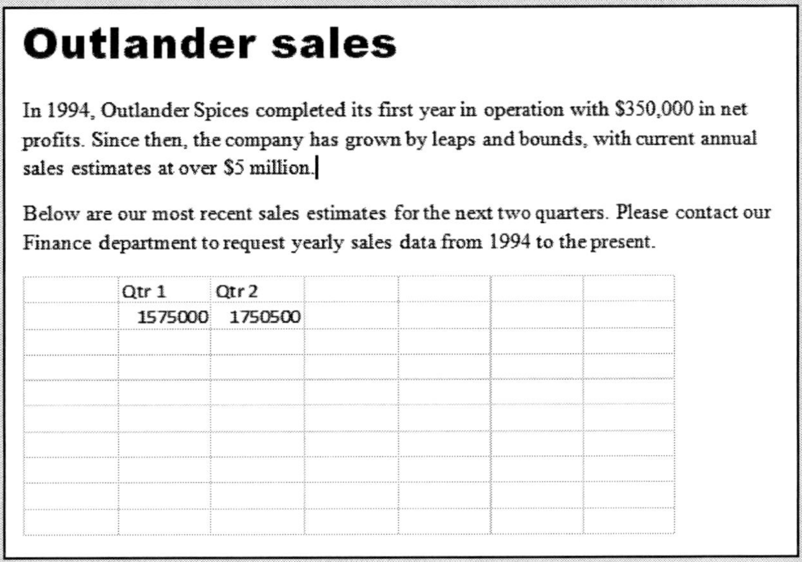

Outlander sales

In 1994, Outlander Spices completed its first year in operation with $350,000 in net profits. Since then, the company has grown by leaps and bounds, with current annual sales estimates at over $5 million.

Below are our most recent sales estimates for the next two quarters. Please contact our Finance department to request yearly sales data from 1994 to the present.

	Qtr 1	Qtr 2
	1575000	1750500

		The Excel data appears below the document text. You can continue working with the Excel data at any time.
12	Double-click the worksheet object	To display it in the Excel environment. You could continue modifying the data.
	Click within the Word document text	To return to the Word environment.
13	Update and close the file	

Inserting existing files as objects

Explanation

In addition to creating objects in Word, you can insert existing files as objects. The file you insert in the Word document is referred to as the *source file*. When you insert a source file as an object, it is embedded in the Word document by default. An *embedded object* is stored in the Word document and is separate from the source file. Changes you make in the source file are not reflected in the embedded version in the Word document.

If you want source-file changes to be reflected in the version you inserted in the Word document, you *link* the object rather than embed it. You can then open the source file from within Word by double-clicking the linked object.

To insert a file as an object:

1 Open the Word document in which you want to add the object, and place the insertion point where you want the object to appear.
2 Click the Insert tab.
3 Click Object to open the Object dialog box.
4 Click the Create from File tab.
5 Click Browse to open the Browse dialog box. Select the file you want to insert, and click Insert.
6 In the Object dialog box, if you want the inserted file to be linked, check "Link to file," as shown in Exhibit 2-2. Otherwise, the content will be embedded.
7 Click OK.

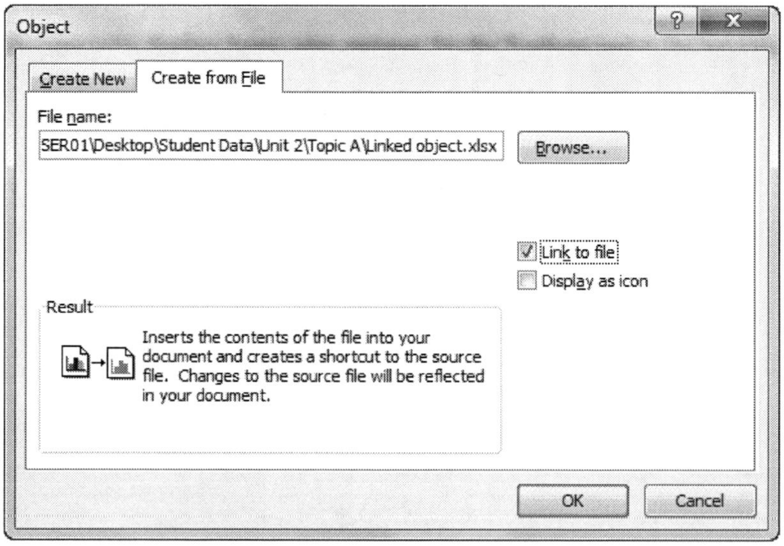

Exhibit 2-2: Inserting a file as a linked object

Do it!

A-2: Inserting an Excel file as a linked object

The files for this activity are in Student Data folder **Unit 2\Topic A**.

Here's how	Here's why
1 Open Objects from files	
Save the document as **My objects from files**	You'll insert an Excel worksheet as an object within this file.
2 Click below the document text	
3 Click the **Insert** tab	
4 Open the Object dialog box	In the Text group, click Object.
Click the **Create from File** tab	
5 Click **Browse**	To open the Browse dialog box.
In the current topic folder, select **Linked object**	This is the Excel file you want to insert as an object.
Click **Insert**	To return to the Object dialog box. The File name box displays the name of the file you chose.
6 Check **Link to file**	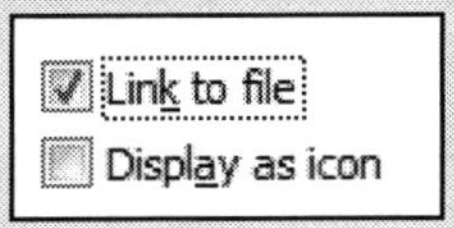 To link the object to the source file.
Click **OK**	The linked object appears below the Word text. If you work in the source file in Excel later, the changes will be reflected in this linked version. You can open the source file from within Word by double-clicking the linked object.
7 Double-click the object	The worksheet opens in an Excel window.
8 Click the total in cell G9	(If necessary.) To select it.
Press CTRL + B	To apply bold formatting.
9 Update the file in Excel	Click the Save button on the Quick Access toolbar.
Close the Excel window	To return to Word.
10 Right-click the Excel object and choose **Update Link**	The linked object reflects the change you made in the source file.
11 Update and close the file	

Inserting charts

Explanation

Another type of object you can insert into a Word document is an Excel chart. Charts are useful for displaying numeric data in a graphic form. When you insert a chart, it is created based on data in an Excel worksheet, as shown in Exhibit 2-3. If you update the Excel worksheet data, the chart in Word will automatically be updated as well.

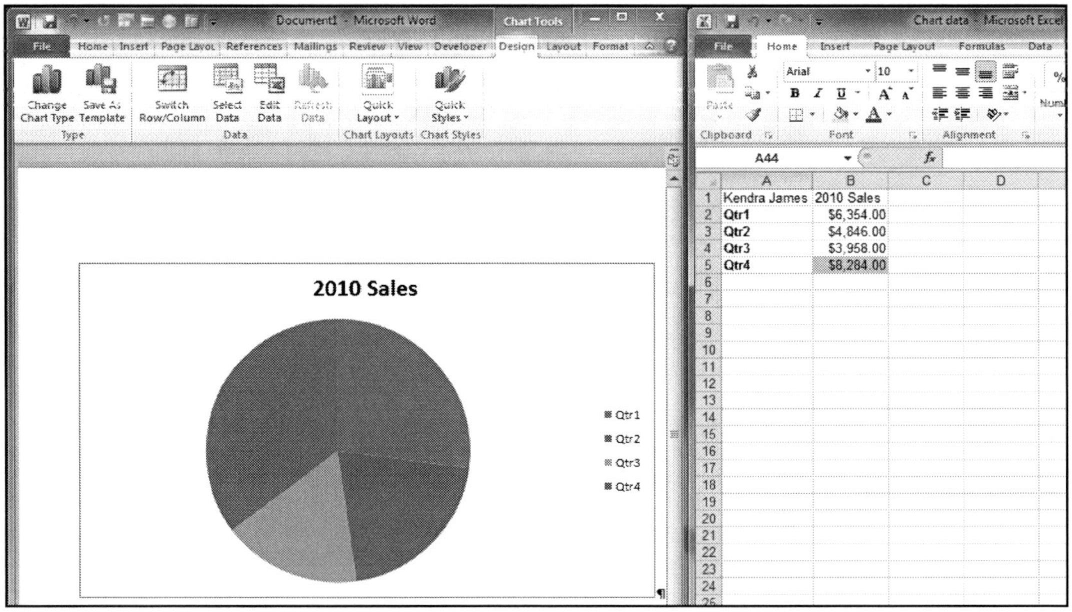

Exhibit 2-3: An Excel chart object in Word

To insert a chart based on new Excel data:

1. In Word, click the Insert tab.
2. In the Illustrations group, click Chart to open the Create Chart dialog box.
3. Select a chart type and click OK. Excel opens, displaying a worksheet with sample data. A chart appears in Word, based on the sample Excel worksheet.
4. In the worksheet, replace the sample data with your own data. The chart will be automatically updated based on the new data.

To insert a chart based on existing Excel data:

1. In Word, click the Insert tab. Click Chart to open the Create Chart dialog box.
2. Select a chart type and click OK. Excel opens, displaying a worksheet with sample data. A chart appears in Word, based on the sample Excel worksheet.
3. In Excel, open the worksheet on which you want to base the chart.
4. In Word, click the Chart Tools | Design tab, if necessary. Then, in the Data group, click Select Data to open the Select Data Source dialog box.
5. In the Excel worksheet that you want to use for the chart, drag to select the range of cells you want to use.
6. Click OK.

In the future, each time you want to further edit the Excel worksheet values, you can open the worksheet by clicking Edit Data Source in Word.

To adjust the layout of the chart in Word, click the Layout tab and specify options such as legend position and data labels.

Do it!

A-3: Inserting a chart based on Excel data

The files for this activity are in Student Data folder **Unit 2\Topic A**.

Here's how	Here's why
1 In Word, create a new blank document	You'll insert a pie chart into this document.
2 Click the **Insert** tab	
3 In the Illustrations group, click **Chart**	To open the Create Chart dialog box.
In the left pane, select **Pie**	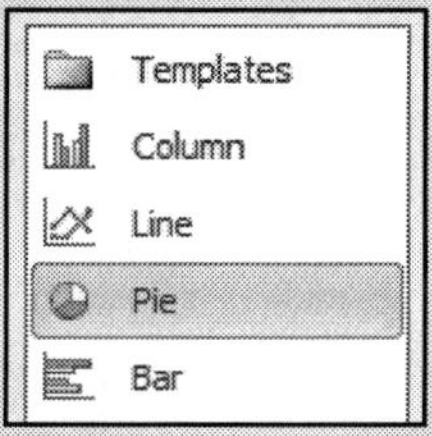
Click **OK**	Excel starts and displays sample data. You'll replace the sample data with data from a file.
4 In Excel, click the **File** tab and click **Open**	The Open dialog box is displayed.
In the current topic folder, select **Chart data**	
Click **Open**	To open the file.
5 In Word, on the Chart Tools | Design tab, click **Select Data**	(In the Data group.) To open the Select Data Source dialog box. In Excel, the sample-data worksheet is activated. You'll specify a range in the Chart data file you opened.
6 In Excel, switch to the Chart data worksheet you opened	Select it on the Windows taskbar.
Drag to select cells A1 through B5	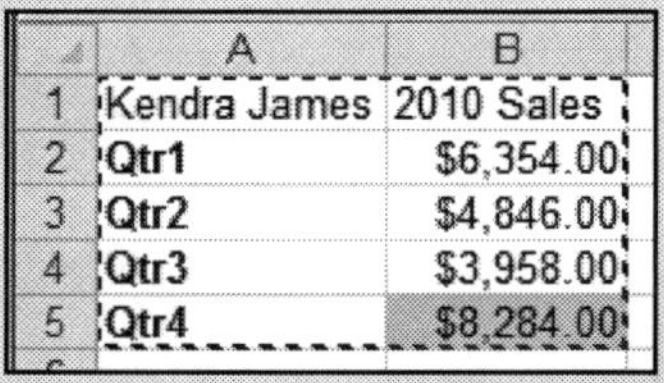 This selection identifies the data to be used to create the chart.
Click **OK**	To close the Select Data Source dialog box and set the data selection. The chart reflects the new data. Use the horizontal scrollbar in the Word window to view the pie chart.

7	In Excel, switch to the Chart data worksheet	(If necessary.) You'll change one of the values in the spreadsheet, and it will automatically change in the chart object in Word.
8	Click cell B3	Cell B3 contains the value $4,846.00.
	Type **7500**	To specify a new value, replacing the old value.
	Observe the chart in Word and press ENTER	When you enter the new value in the Excel worksheet, the chart in Word is updated as well.
9	In Excel, save Chart data as **My chart data** and close all open worksheets	Click the File tab and click Save As. Save the file. Then click the File tab and click Close.
	Close Excel	
10	In Word, save the document as **My chart**	In the current topic folder.
11	Click the **Layout** tab	
	In the Labels group, click **Legend** and select **Show Legend at Top**	To adjust the layout.
	Click **Data Labels** and select **Center**	To display the data values in the chart.
12	Click the **Design** tab	You'll save the chart as a template.
	In the Type group, click **Save As Template**	To open the Save Chart Template dialog box.
	Edit the File name box to read **My sales template**	
	Click **Save**	
	Update and close the document	

Topic B: Changing the document background

This topic covers the following Microsoft Office Specialist objectives for exam 77-881: Word 2010.

#	Objective
3.2	**Apply themes**
	3.2.1 Use a theme to apply formatting
	3.2.2 Customize a theme
3.3	**Construct content in a document by using the Quick Parts tool**
	3.3.1 Add built-in building blocks
	3.3.1.6 Watermark
3.4	**Create and manipulate page backgrounds**
	3.4.1 Format a document's background
	3.4.2 Set a colored background
	3.4.3 Add a watermark
	3.4.4 Set page borders

This topic covers the following Microsoft Office Specialist objectives for exam 77-887: Word Expert 2010.

#	Objective
1.1	**Configure Word options**
	1.1.1 Change default program options
1.2	**Apply protection to a document**
	1.2.1 Restrict editing

Document backgrounds

Explanation

You can customize the background of a document by using background colors and fill effects, watermarks, or themes. A *watermark* is any text or image that can be seen behind the text in a document. For example, an organization's letterhead might have the company logo as a watermark. *Themes* contain styles and background colors you can use for a consistent look among your documents.

Background colors

To add a background color to a document, click the Page Layout tab. In the Page Background group, click Page Color and select a color swatch.

You can also apply special effects to the background. To do this, use the tabs in the Fill Effects dialog box, shown in Exhibit 2-4. These tabs are described in the following table.

Tab	Used to...
Gradient	Apply multiple colors, which blend from one to another, as a background. Also used to apply various shading styles.
Texture	Select the texture with which the color can be filled.
Pattern	Select the pattern—such as dotted, line, or bars—in which the background color can appear.
Picture	Apply a picture as the background.

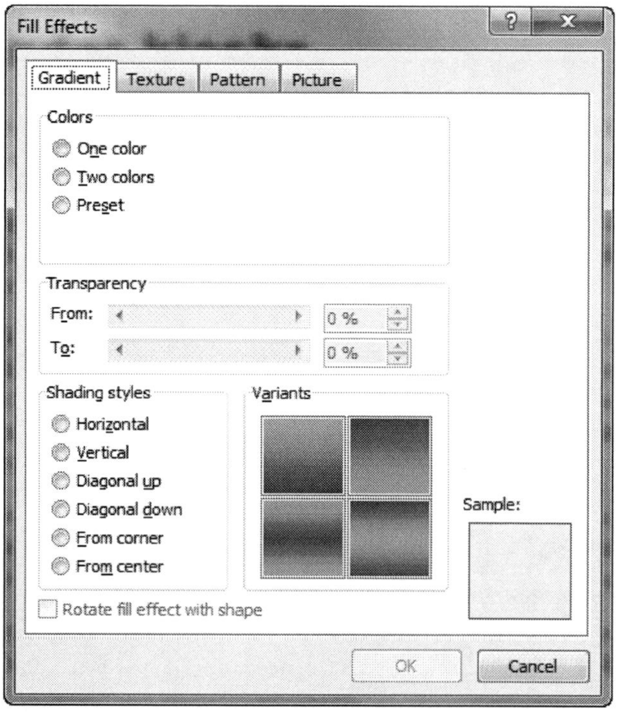

Exhibit 2-4: The Fill Effects dialog box

To apply background gradients, textures, patterns, or pictures to a document:

1. Click the Page Layout tab.
2. Click Page Color and choose Fill Effects to open the Fill Effects dialog box.
3. Use the Gradient, Texture, Pattern, and Picture tabs to specify the desired effects.
4. Click OK.

Page borders

To enhance the appearance of a document, you might want to add a border to one or more pages. To do so, click the Page Layout tab and click Page Borders in the Page Background group. In the Borders and Shading dialog box, select and customize the border. By default, page borders are applied to all pages in a document, but you can apply them to only specific sections.

Do it!

B-1: Adding background colors, fill effects, and borders

The files for this activity are in Student Data folder **Unit 2\Topic B**.

Here's how	Here's why
1 Open Backgrounds	If necessary, maximize the window.
Save the document as **My backgrounds**	
2 Click the **Page Layout** tab	
3 In the Page Background group, click **Page Color**	 To display the Color gallery.
4 Select the Light Green color, as shown	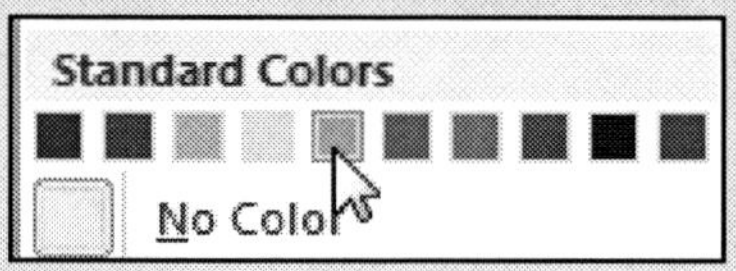 To apply light green as the document's background color. Next, you'll apply a gradient.
5 Click **Page Color** and choose **Fill Effects…**	(In the Page Background group.) To open the Fill Effects dialog box.
Under Colors, select **One color**	You'll combine the green background color with a lighter shade of the same color.
Drag the Dark Light slider close to the right end of the bar, as shown	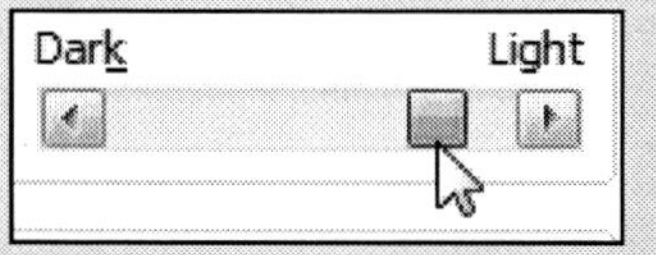 To specify a lighter shade of the green color. If you drag all the way to the right, the green color will blend with white.
6 Under Shading styles, select **Diagonal down**	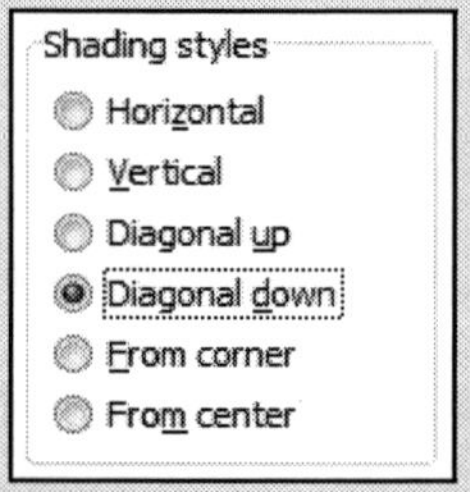 Four Diagonal down options appear below Variants.

7 Under Variants, select the top-right option, as shown

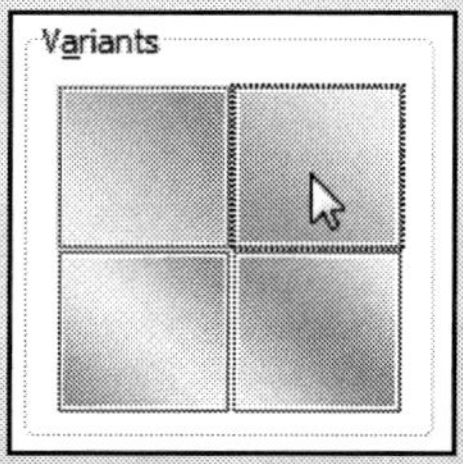

Click **OK**

To close the Fill Effects dialog box and apply the selected shading style.

8 Open the Fill Effects dialog box

In the Page Background group, click Page Color and choose Fill Effects.

Click the **Texture** tab

Select the **Parchment** option, as shown

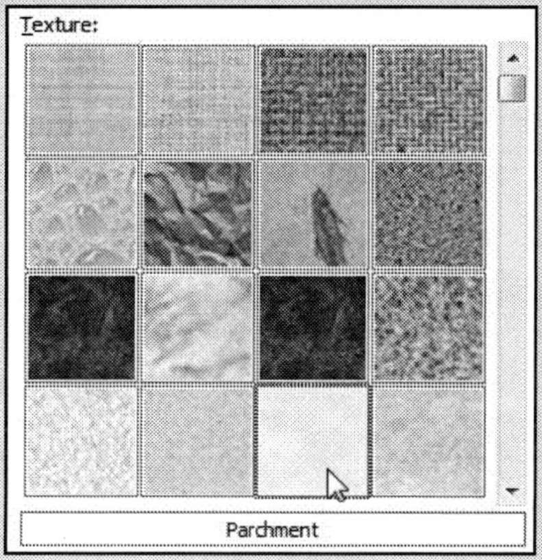

Click **OK**

To replace the previous background with a background texture that resembles parchment paper.

9 In the Page Background group, click **Page Borders**

To open the Borders and Shading dialog box.

Under Setting, click as shown

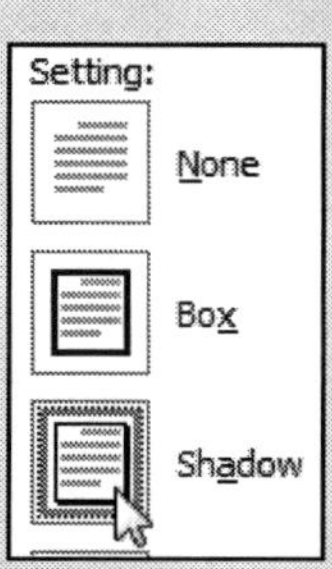

To select the Shadow page border. in the Apply to list, Whole document is selected by default.

Click **OK**

To add the page border to the document.

10 Update and close the document

Watermarks

Explanation

You can add text or a picture as a document's watermark. To add a text watermark:

1. Click the Page Layout tab.
2. In the Page Background group, click Watermark and choose Custom Watermark to open the Printed Watermark dialog box.
3. Select Text watermark.
4. From the Text list, select the text you want to use as the watermark, or enter your own text in the Text box.
5. Format the text by using the Font, Size, and Color lists.
6. Click Apply to preview the watermark. Click Close.

To add a picture watermark, select the Picture watermark option in the Printed Watermark dialog box.

Exhibit 2-5 shows some of the watermarks available in Word.

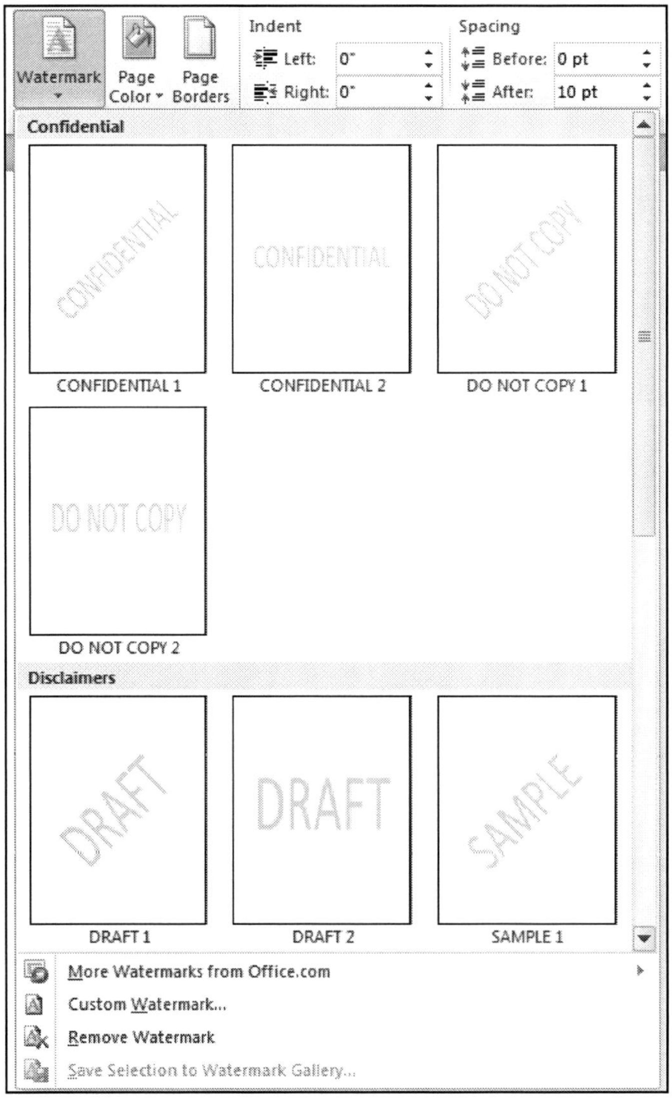

Exhibit 2-5: Text watermarks

Do it!

B-2: Adding a watermark

The files for this activity are in Student Data folder **Unit 2\Topic B**.

Here's how	Here's why
1 Open Watermark	
Save the document as **My watermark**	This document is a sample from a forthcoming recipe book. You'll add a watermark to identify its status to anyone who opens it.
2 Click the **Page Layout** tab	
3 In the Page Background group, click **Watermark** and choose **Custom Watermark...**	 To open the Printed Watermark dialog box.
4 Select **Text watermark**	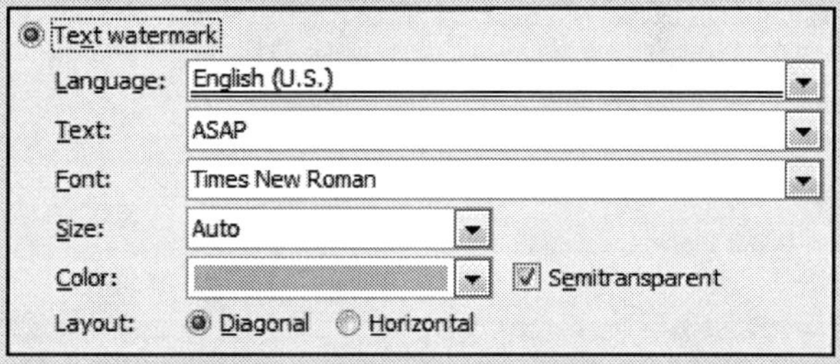 The text and font options are now available.
5 From the Text list, select **SAMPLE**	(Scroll down in the list.) To specify "SAMPLE" as the text that will appear in the background of the document.
From the Font list, select **Arial Black**	(Scroll up in the list.) To change the font. You can also specify a size for the text, but here, you'll use the Auto default setting.
Click **Apply**	To preview the watermark on the document page.
6 Click **Close**	To close the dialog box. The SAMPLE watermark appears diagonally behind the text on every page.
7 Scroll to view the document pages	To verify that the watermark appears on each page.
8 Update and close the document	

Themes

Explanation

A *theme* is a named set of colors, fonts, and effects that can be applied to all pages in a document to provide a consistent look. When you apply a theme, the page formatting is changed, and the elements—such as background colors, heading styles, and table border colors—are customized based on the characteristics of the theme.

To apply a theme, click the Page Layout tab, click Themes, and select the desired theme from the gallery, shown in Exhibit 2-6. If you want to apply only the colors, only the fonts, or only the effects for a particular theme, you can select options from the appropriate lists in the Themes group. *Theme effects* are graphical properties that are applied to any charts, SmartArt graphics, shapes, or pictures in a document.

If you've specified a theme and have customized it by applying different colors, fonts, and effects, you can save the custom settings by clicking Themes and choosing Save Current Theme.

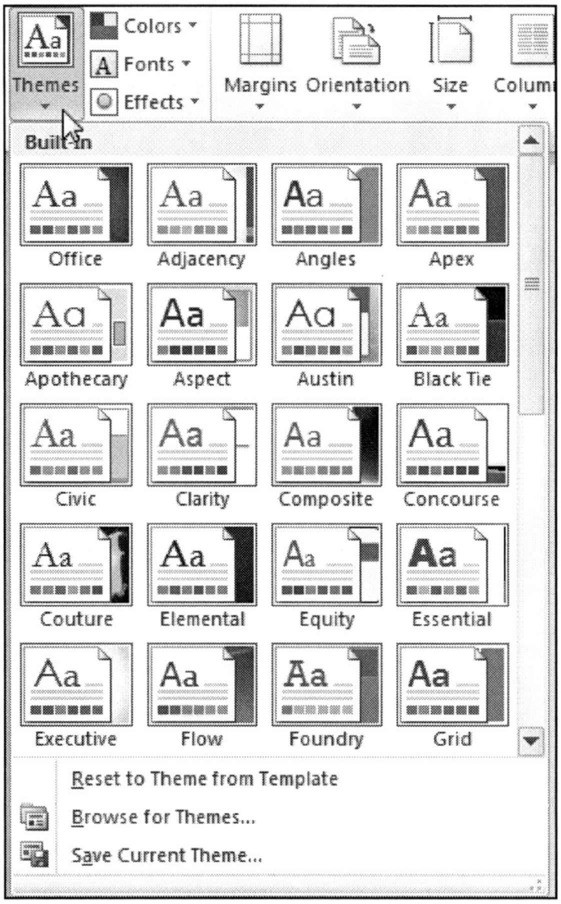

Exhibit 2-6: The Themes gallery

Restoring a template theme

If you change a document's theme, but later decide that you'd like to return to the original theme attributes, you can restore the original template theme. To do so, click Themes on the Page Layout tab and choose Reset to Theme from Template.

Do it!

B-3: Applying themes

The files for this activity are in Student Data folder **Unit 2\Topic B**.

Here's how	Here's why
1 Open Themes	
Save the document as **My themes**	You'll use a theme to format this document.
2 Click the **Page Layout** tab	
3 In the Themes group, click **Themes**	To display the Themes gallery.
Point to the Opulent theme, as shown	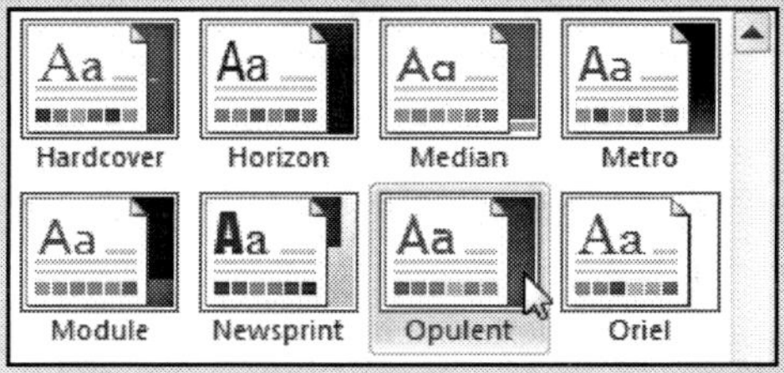 To preview the theme in the document. Notice how the appearance of the document's fonts, colors, and SmartArt changes.
Select a theme	To apply it, changing the overall appearance of the document.
4 In the Themes group, click **Themes**	
Choose **Reset to Theme from Template**	To return to the original theme used in the document's template. Rather than change all document aspects at once (fonts, colors, and graphic properties) with a theme, you can change individual characteristics.
5 In the Themes group, click 	To display a gallery of theme colors. You can select a set of colors from another theme, or customize the colors in the current theme.
Choose **Create New Theme Colors...**	To open the Create New Theme Colors dialog box.

6	From the Text/Background – Light 1 list, select the indicated option	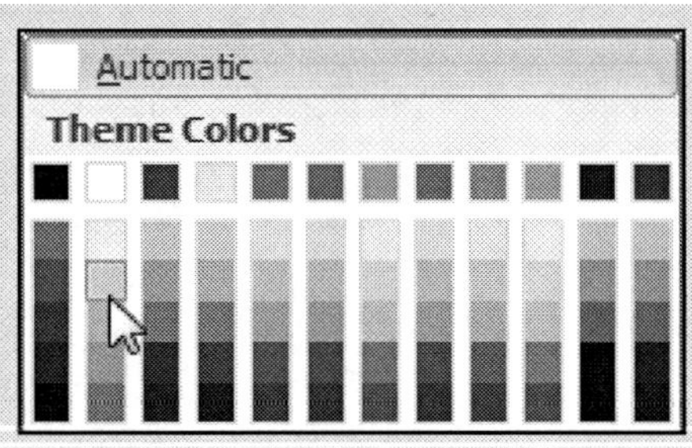
		(White, Text 1, Darker 15%.) To select a different color for all Text/Background – Light 1 document elements.
	Click **Save**	To apply this change. It affects the background color of the SmartArt graphic.
7	In the Themes group, click 	To display a gallery of font sets.
	Select a Theme Font	To modify only the fonts used in the document.
8	In the Themes group, click 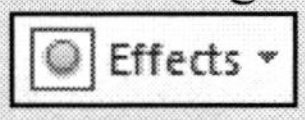	To display a gallery of effects that will be applied to any charts, SmartArt graphics, shapes, or pictures in the document.
	Select **Concourse**	To change the appearance of the SmartArt graphic.
9	Click **Themes** and choose **Save Current Theme...**	To open the Save Current theme dialog box.
	Edit the File name box to read **My theme**	
	Click **Save**	To save the custom theme.
10	Update the file	

Protecting document formatting

Explanation

After you've formatted a document, you might want to protect it so that you or others can't change it. To prevent someone from modifying or using styles or changing a document's theme, you can set formatting restrictions.

To prevent someone from changing a document's theme:

1. On the Review tab, in the Protect group, click Protect Document to open the Restrict Formatting and Editing task pane.
2. Under Formatting restrictions, click Settings to open the Formatting Restrictions dialog box.
3. Under Formatting, check "Block Theme or Scheme switching," as shown in Exhibit 2-7.
4. Click OK.

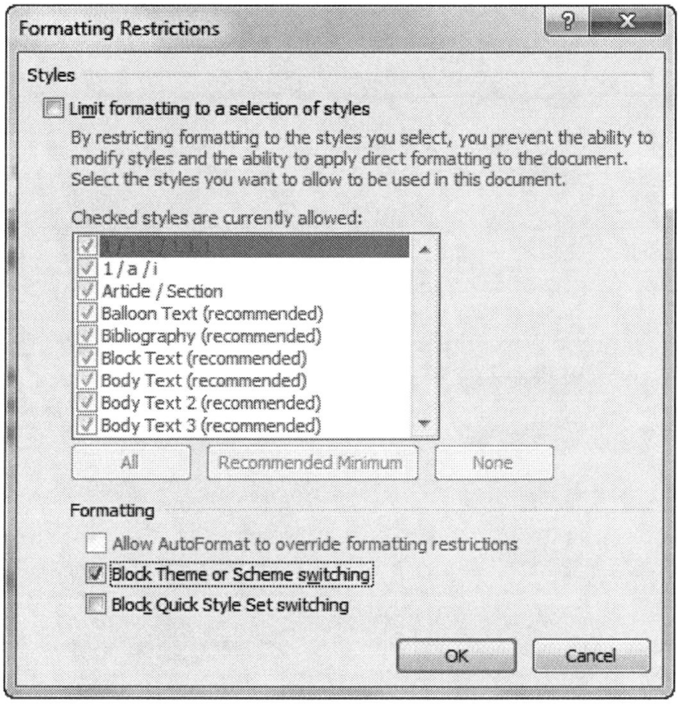

Exhibit 2-7: The Formatting Restrictions dialog box

Do it!

B-4: Protecting a theme

Here's how	Here's why
1 Click the **Review** tab	
In the Protect group, click **Restrict Editing**	 To open the Restrict Formatting and Editing pane.
2 Under "1. Formatting restrictions," click **Settings**	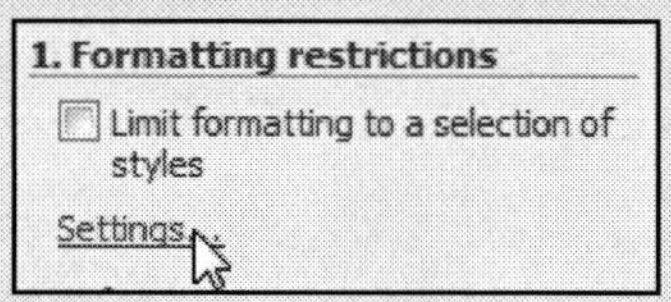 To open the Formatting Restrictions dialog box.
Check **Block Theme or Scheme switching**	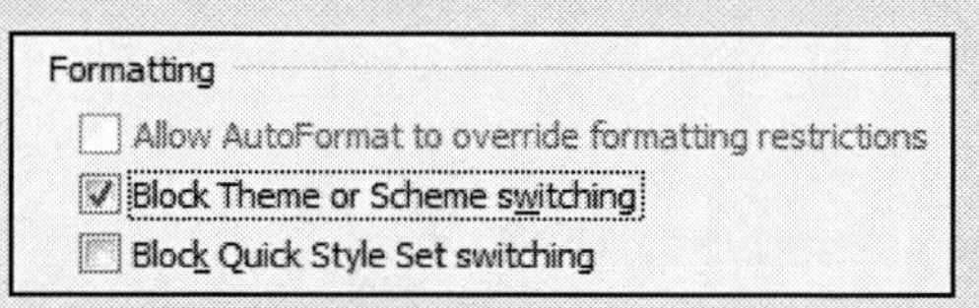
Click **OK**	
3 Click the **Page Layout** tab	
Observe the Themes group	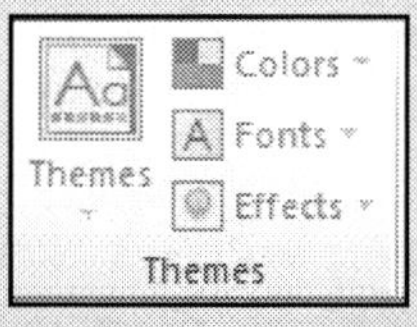 The choices are grayed out. This group is no longer available because you restricted the formatting. Themes and their components can no longer be changed in this document.
4 Open the Formatting Restrictions dialog box	Under Formatting restrictions, click Settings.
Clear **Block Theme or Scheme switching**	To remove the restriction.
Click **OK**	
5 Observe the Themes group	The tools are now available because you removed the restriction.
6 Close the Restrict Formatting and Editing pane	

Specifying a default theme

Explanation

If you use a certain theme most of the time, consider making it your default theme. Then when you create documents, that theme will automatically be applied.

To specify a default theme:

1. On the Page Layout tab, in the Themes group, click Themes to open the gallery.
2. Select the desired theme.
3. On the Home tab, in the Styles group, click Change Styles.
4. Choose Set as Default, as shown in Exhibit 2-8.

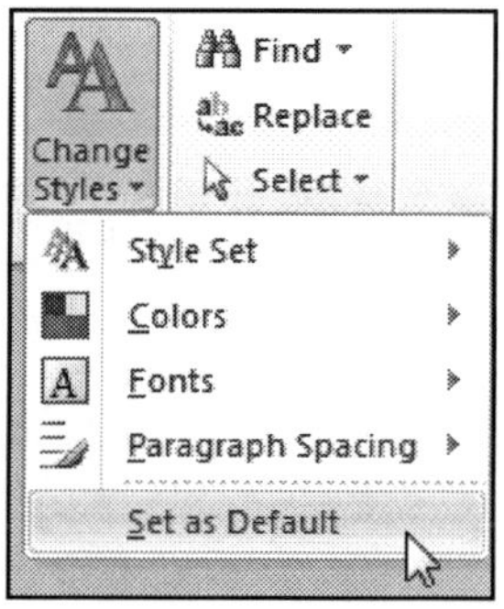

Exhibit 2-8: Setting a default theme

Do it!

B-5: Setting a default theme

Here's how	Here's why
1 In the Themes group, click **Themes**	To display the Themes gallery.
Click **Foundry**	To select the Foundry theme.
2 Click the **Home** tab	
3 In the Styles group, click **Change Styles**	
Choose **Set as Default**	To set the Foundry theme as the default. Now when you create a document, it will automatically have the Foundry theme applied.
4 Update and close the file	
5 Create a new blank document	
6 Enter **Outlander Spices**	To create a document heading.
Apply the **Heading 1** style to the text	 The appearance of the text is defined by the Foundry theme.
7 Click the **Page Layout** tab	
Click **Themes**	The selected theme is Foundry.
8 Change the document theme to **Office**	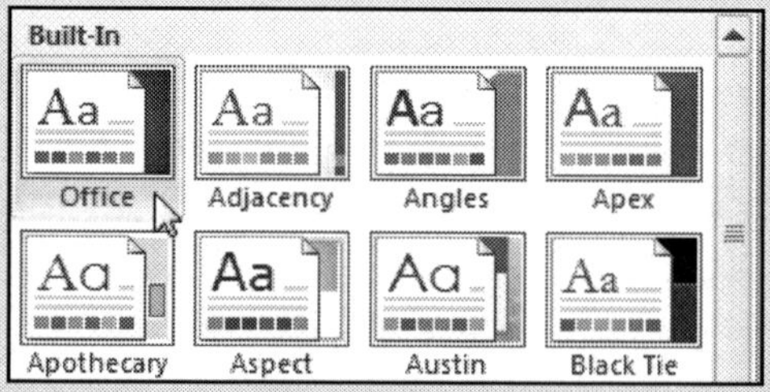 On the Page Layout tab, click Themes and select Office.
9 Set the Office theme as the default	On the Home tab, click Change Styles and choose Set as Default.
Close the file without saving	

Unit summary: Objects and backgrounds

Topic A In this topic, you created an Excel worksheet object in a Word document. You also inserted an Excel file as a **linked object**, modified the data, and inserted an Excel chart as an object in your Word document.

Topic B In this topic, you learned how to apply **background** colors and **fill effects** to a document. You also created a **watermark**. In addition, you learned about **themes** and how they can be used to create a consistent look throughout a document.

Independent practice activity

In this activity, you'll apply a theme to a document, and you'll insert one document into another as a linked object.

The files for this activity are in Student Data folder **Unit 2\Unit summary**.

1. Open Update and save it as **My update**.
2. Apply the Technic theme to the document. (*Hint:* Use the Themes group on the Page Layout tab.)
3. Change the page color to a color of your choice. (*Hint:* Use the Page Color button in the Page Background group.)
4. Update and close the document.
5. Open Practice objects and save it as **My practice objects**.
6. Below the current document text, insert the **Practice linked object** file as a linked object. (*Hint:* In the Object dialog box, use the Create from File tab.)
7. Open the Practice linked object file in Excel. (*Hint:* Double-click the object to open the original file in Excel.)
8. Apply a light color fill to the cell containing the highest value in the Sales column. (*Hint:* Click cell D4. On the Home tab, click the Fill Color arrow and choose a light color.)
9. Update the document and close Excel.
10. In Word, update the linked object.
11. Update and close the file.

Review questions

1 When you insert a source file as an object in a Word document, what's the difference between linking and embedding the object?

2 How can you apply a solid background color to a document?

3 How can you apply a gradient background to a document?

4 On which Ribbon tab will you find the Watermarks button for adding a watermark?

A Home

B Insert

C Page Layout

D References

5 Which of the following will not be changed when you apply a theme to a document?

A Colors

B Page breaks

C Fonts

D Effects

Unit 3
Using macros

Unit time: 40 minutes

Complete this unit, and you'll know how to:

A Record and run macros to automate tasks.

B Modify, copy, and delete macros.

Topic A: Recording and running macros

This topic covers the following Microsoft Office Specialist objectives for exam 77-887: Word Expert 2010.

#	Objective	
5.1	**Apply and manipulate macros**	
	5.1.1	Record a macro
	5.1.2	Run a macro
	5.1.3	Apply macro security
5.2	**Apply and manipulate macro options**	
	5.2.1	Run macros when a document is opened
	5.2.2	Run macros when a button is clicked
	5.2.3	Assign a macro to a command button
	5.2.4	Create a custom macro button on the Quick Access Toolbar

Working with macros

Explanation

While working in Word, you might have to perform repetitive tasks—for example, inserting or formatting tables that you use often. A *macro* is a collection of actions used to automate complicated, lengthy, or repetitive tasks. There are two ways to create a macro. The easiest method is to use the *macro recorder* to identify the actions. The other method is to enter Visual Basic code in the Microsoft Visual Basic for Applications editor.

Creating macros

To create a macro by using the macro recorder:

1. On the View tab, in the Macros group, click Macros and choose Record Macro to open the Record Macro dialog box, shown in Exhibit 3-1.
2. In the Macro name box, enter a name for the macro.
3. Using the "Store macro in" list, specify whether you want to store the macro in the current document only or make the macro available for all documents.
4. In the Description box, enter a description of the macro.
5. *(Optional)* Create a macro button on the Quick Access toolbar or assign a keyboard shortcut to the macro.
   - Click Button to open the Word Options dialog box. Under "Choose commands from," select the macro and click Add. Click Modify to edit the button's icon. Click OK to close the dialog box.
   - Click Keyboard to open the Customize Keyboard dialog box. Press the desired keys to enter the shortcut in the "Press new shortcut key" box. Click Assign, and then click Close to close the dialog box.
6. Click OK to close the Record Macro dialog box.

7 Perform the steps that you want to store in this macro. As you work, Word records your actions. At any time, you can click Macros and choose Pause Recording; when you're ready to start again, click Macros and choose Resume Recorder.

8 When you're done, click Macros and choose Stop Recording.

You can also enable the Developer tab and use the commands in the Code group to record and edit macros.

Quick access Toolbar

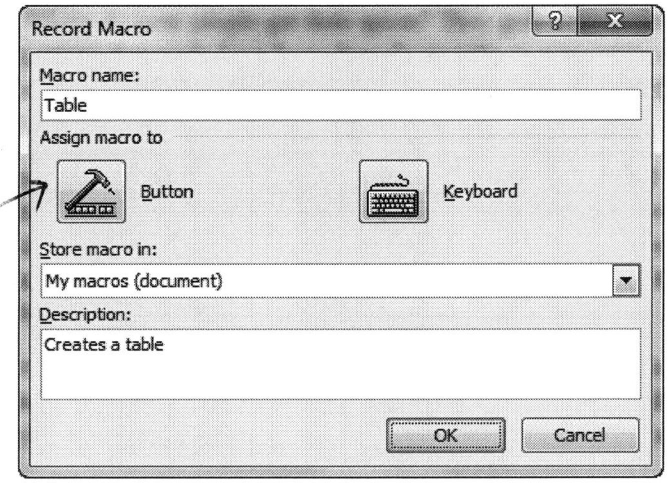

Exhibit 3-1: The Record Macro dialog box

Do it!

A-1: Recording a macro

The files for this activity are in Student Data folder **Unit 3\Topic A**.

Here's how	Here's why
1 Open Macros	You'll record a macro to create a table.
Save the document as **My macros**	In the current topic folder.
2 Place the insertion point at the end of the document	(Press Ctrl+End.) Below the heading "New kiosk locations."
3 Click the **View** tab	
4 Click **Macros** as shown	
Choose **Record Macro...**	To open the Record Macro dialog box.
5 Edit the Macro name box to read **Table**	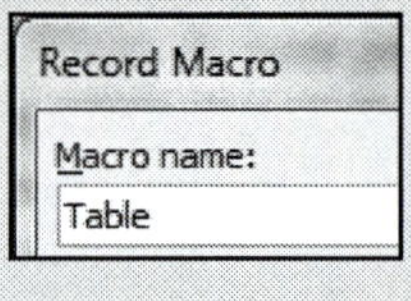 To specify a name for the macro.
6 From the "Store macro in" list, select **My macros (document)**	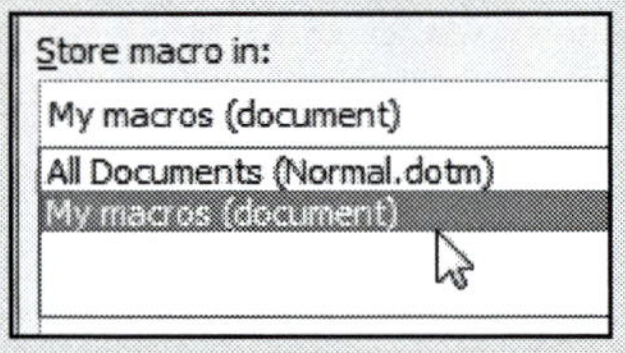 The macro will be available in only this document.
7 In the Description box, enter **Creates a table**	To describe the macro. Your Record Macro dialog box should match Exhibit 3-1.
8 Click 	To open the Word Options dialog box. You'll add a custom macro button to the Quick Access toolbar.
Select **Project.NewMacros.Table**	
Click **Add** and click **OK**	 The image of a cassette is attached to the pointer. In addition, a custom macro button appears on the Quick Access toolbar.

9 Click the **Insert** tab

You'll go through the steps of inserting a table, and the macro will record those steps.

10 In the Tables group, click **Table** and select the indicated cells

To insert a table with three columns and two rows.

11 Verify that the insertion point is in the first cell of the table

The upper-left cell.

Press SHIFT + → three times

To select the top row of the table.

Press CTRL + B

To apply bold formatting to the top row.

12 On the View tab, click **Macros** and choose **Stop Recording**

To stop recording the macro.

13 Update the document

A dialog box appears, stating that you can't save the macro with this file because this file is a macro-free document.

Click **No**

To cancel the update. The Save As dialog box appears. You'll save the document as a macro-enabled document, with the extension .docm.

14 From the Save as type list, select **Word Macro-Enabled Document**

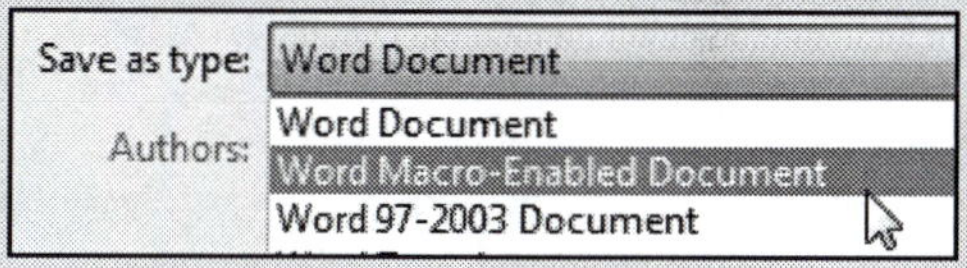

Click **Save**

Viewing macro scripts

Explanation

When you create a macro by using the recorder, your steps are translated into Visual Basic code. You can view and edit this code in the Microsoft Visual Basic for Applications editor. The macro code starts with a `Sub` statement followed by the macro name, and ends with an `End Sub` statement.

The code can include comment entries. For example, you can add the name and description of a macro as comments in the macro code. Well-written comments can be helpful in understanding or debugging the macro. When the code executes, Word ignores these comment entries.

To view a macro's code:

1. On the View tab, in the Macros group, click the top portion of the Macros button to open the Macros dialog box.
2. In the Macro name box, select the desired macro.
3. Click Edit to open the Microsoft Visual Basic for Applications editor, shown in Exhibit 3-2.

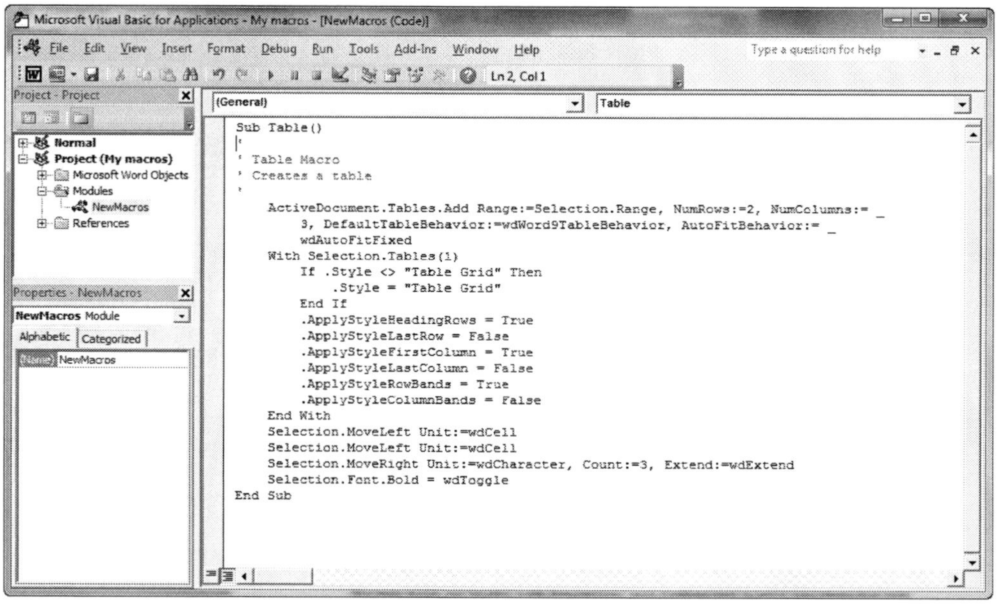

Exhibit 3-2: The Microsoft Visual Basic for Applications window

Do it!

A-2: Viewing a macro script

Here's how	Here's why
1 In the Macros group, click 	(The top part of the Macros button.) To open the Macros dialog box. In the Macro name box, Table is selected.
2 In the list of macros, select **Table**	(If necessary.) To select the macro you want to view.
Click **Edit**	To view the macro script in the Microsoft Visual Basic for Applications editor, as shown in Exhibit 3-2.
3 Choose **File**, **Close and Return to Microsoft Word**	To close the Microsoft Visual Basic for Applications editor.

Running macros

Explanation

By default, you can run macros from only trusted sources, and unsigned macros are automatically disabled. When you open a document containing an unsigned macro, such as those created in this course, a Security Warning message appears below the Ribbon. If you want to enable the document's unsigned macros, click Enable Content.

To change how Word deals with documents containing macros, you can change Word's security settings. To do so:

1. On the File tab, click Options to open the Word Options dialog box.
2. Click Trust Center; then click Trust Center Settings to open the Trust Center dialog box.
3. Click Macro Settings.
4. Select a macro security setting, as shown in Exhibit 3-3.
5. Click OK. All documents you open will now adhere to the new security setting.

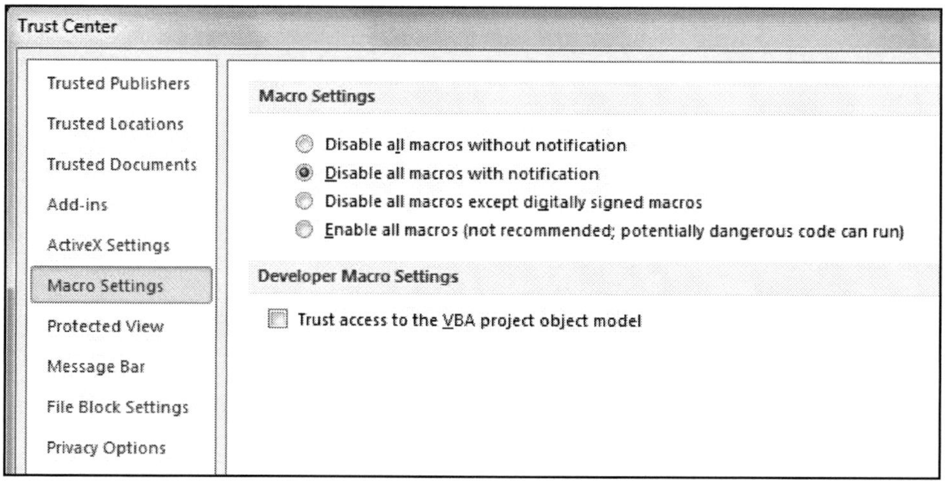

Exhibit 3-3: The Macro Settings in the Trust Center dialog box

To run a macro:

1. On the View tab, click the top part of the Macros button to open the Macros dialog box. You can also press Alt+F8.
2. From the Macros in list, select the document or template where the macro is stored.
3. Select the macro you want to run, as shown in Exhibit 3-4.
4. Click Run.

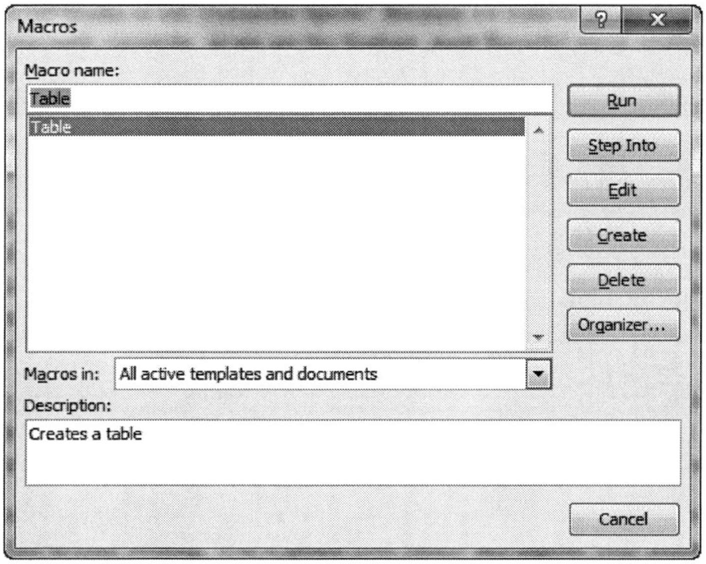

Exhibit 3-4: The Macros dialog box

If you added a custom macro button to the Quick Access toolbar when you created a macro, you can click the button to run the macro.

In addition, you can create a command button on the Ribbon that you can click to run a macro. To do so:

1 Open the Word Options dialog box.
2 Click Customize Ribbon.
3 Under "Customize the Ribbon," select the tab on which you want to add the macro, and then click New Group. Click Rename and enter a custom name for the group.
4 From the "Choose commands from" list, select Macros.
5 Select the macro you want to add as a command button and click Add to add it to your custom group.
6 Click OK.

You can also specify that a macro will run when you open a document. To do so, change the macro's name to AutoOpen. When you open a document that uses a template containing the AutoOpen macro, the macro will run automatically.

Do it!

A-3: Running a macro

Here's how	Here's why
1 On the File tab, click **Options**	To open the Word Options dialog box.
Click **Trust Center**	
Click **Trust Center Settings**	To open the Trust Center dialog box.
Click **Macro Settings**	
2 Observe the current macro security setting	This default setting, shown in Exhibit 3-3, disables all macros, but displays a security alert when macros are present. It allows you to enable macros on a case-by-case basis.
Click **Cancel**	To close the Trust Center dialog box.
Click **Cancel**	To close the Word Options dialog box.
3 Close the document	
4 Open the macro-enabled version of My macros	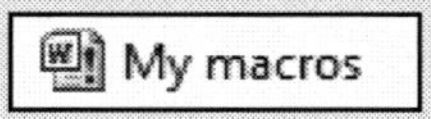 The icon is displayed with an exclamation point, and the tooltip displays "Type: Microsoft Word Macro-Enabled Document."
Observe the Security Warning	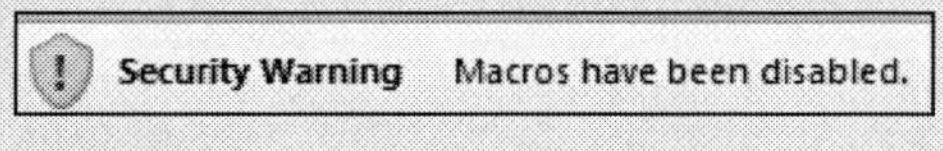
5 Click **Enable Content**	
6 Place the insertion point at the end of the document, and press ENTER	You'll insert a table here.
7 On the Quick Access toolbar, click 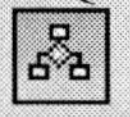	(The custom macro button you added.) To run the macro that inserts a table with three columns and two rows. The first row has been formatted to appear in bold text.
8 Update and close the document	

Topic B: Modifying and deleting macros

Explanation

After you create a macro, you can edit it by opening it in the Microsoft Visual Basic for Applications editor. For example, you can modify a macro that creates a three-column table so that it creates a ten-column table instead.

To modify a macro:

1. On the View tab, click the top part of the Macros button to open the Macros dialog box.
2. In the list of macros, select the one you want to edit.
3. Click Edit to open the Microsoft Visual Basic for Applications editor.
4. Edit the code as needed.
5. Close the Microsoft Visual Basic for Applications editor.

```
Sub Table()
'
' Table Macro
' Creates a table
'
    ActiveDocument.Tables.Add Range:=Selection.Range, NumRows:=10, NumColumns:= _
        3, DefaultTableBehavior:=wdWord9TableBehavior, AutoFitBehavior:= _
        wdAutoFitFixed
    With Selection.Tables(1)
        If .Style <> "Table Grid" Then
            .Style = "Table Grid"
        End If
        .ApplyStyleHeadingRows = True
        .ApplyStyleLastRow = False
        .ApplyStyleFirstColumn = True
        .ApplyStyleLastColumn = False
        .ApplyStyleRowBands = True
        .ApplyStyleColumnBands = False
    End With
    Selection.MoveLeft Unit:=wdCell
    Selection.MoveRight Unit:=wdCharacter, Count:=3, Extend:=wdExtend
    Selection.Font.Bold = wdToggle
End Sub
```

Exhibit 3-5: Editing a macro

Do it!

B-1: Modifying a macro

The files for this activity are in Student Data folder **Unit 3\Topic B**.

Here's how	Here's why
1 Open Macros complete	
Click **Enable Content**	To enable macros in this document.
2 Save the document as **My macros complete**	
3 Open the Macros dialog box	On the View tab, click the top part of the Macros button.
Click **Edit**	To open Microsoft Visual Basic for Applications.
4 Edit the code as shown	`NumRows:=10,` (Located in the line of code that begins with `ActiveDocument.Tables.Add Range`.) To increase the number of rows in the table from two to 10.
Close Microsoft Visual Basic for Applications	Choose File, Close and Return to Microsoft Word.
5 Place the insertion point at the end of the document	
6 Run the **Table** macro	(Click the button on the Quick Access toolbar.) A table with three columns and 10 rows is added to the document. You might need to scroll to see the entire table.
7 Update the document	

Copying macros

Explanation

After you create a macro that is stored in a single document, you might want to copy it to other files or templates. To copy a macro between files:

1. Open both the file containing the macro to be copied and the destination file.
2. Activate the document containing the macro, and open the Macros dialog box.
3. Click Organizer to open the Organizer dialog box with the Macro Project Items tab active, as shown in Exhibit 3-6.
4. From the “Macro Project Items available in” list on the left side, select the file or template containing the macro you want to copy.
5. From the “Macro Project Items available in” list on the right side, select the file or template to which you want to copy the macro. If the file is not available in the list, click Close File and then click Open File to display the Open dialog box. From the Open dialog box, open the file you want.
6. From the In *<file-name>* list (where *<file-name>* represents the name of the document), select the macro to be copied.
7. Click Copy.
8. Click Close to close the Organizer dialog box.

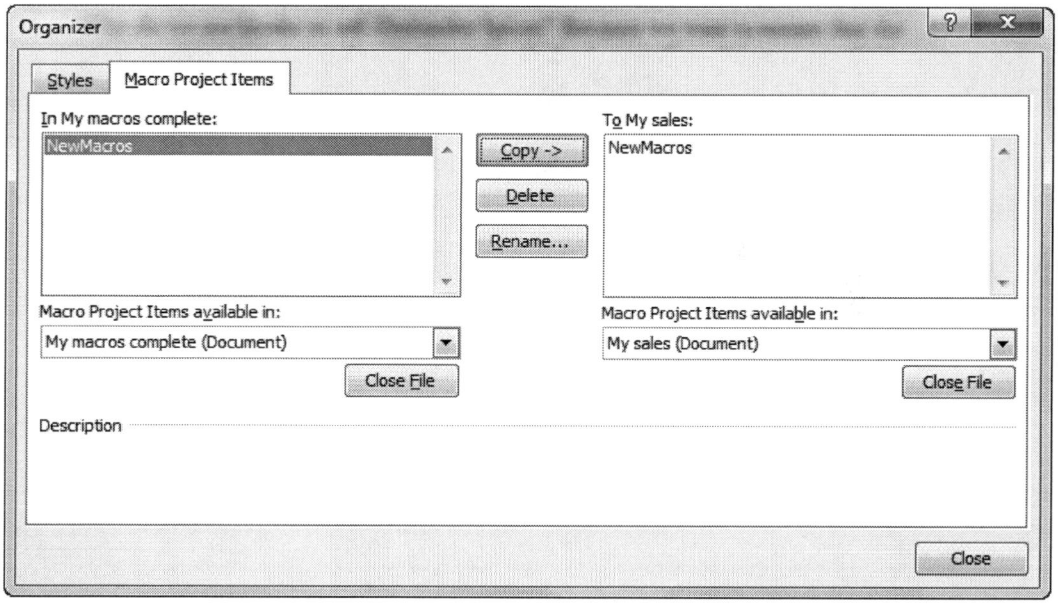

Exhibit 3-6: The Organizer dialog box

Do it!

B-2: Copying a macro

The files for this activity are in Student Data folder **Unit 3\Topic B**.

Here's how	Here's why
1 Open Sales	You'll copy the Table macro to this document.
Save the document as **My sales**	This document is already a Word macro-enabled document.
2 Activate the "My macros complete" document window	Click its button in the Windows taskbar.
3 Open the Macros dialog box	
Click **Organizer**	To open the Organizer dialog box.
Observe the "In My macros complete" list	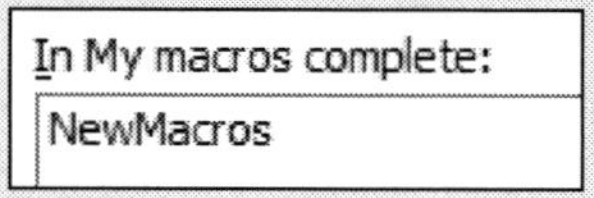 NewMacros appears in the list. You'll copy this macro.
4 On the right side of the Organizer, click **Close File**	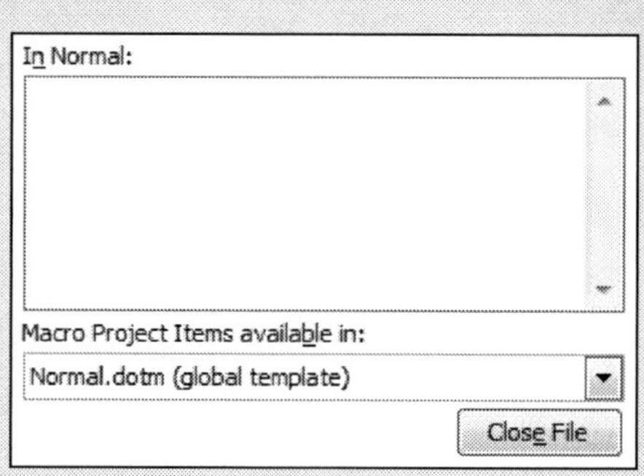 The button name changes to Open File.
5 Click **Open File**	The Open dialog box appears.
Navigate to the current topic folder	Student Data folder Unit 3\Topic B.
From the file types list, select **All Word Documents**	
Select **My sales** and click **Open**	To designate My sales as the target file in the Organizer dialog box.
6 Click **Copy**	To copy the macro from My macros to My sales. Your Organizer dialog box should match Exhibit 3-4.
7 Click **Close**	To close the Organizer dialog box.
8 Activate the "My sales" document window	

9	Place the insertion point at the end of the document	You'll run the macro to insert a table below the document text.
10	Open the Macros dialog box	The Table macro has been copied and is available.
	Click **Run**	To run the macro, inserting a table with 10 rows.
11	Update and close My sales	Save the file as a macro-enabled document, if prompted.

Deleting macros

Explanation

If a macro becomes obsolete, you can delete it by using the Macros dialog box. To do so:

1. Open the Macros dialog box.
2. Select the macro you want to delete.
3. Click Delete. A message box asks you to confirm the action.
4. Click Yes.

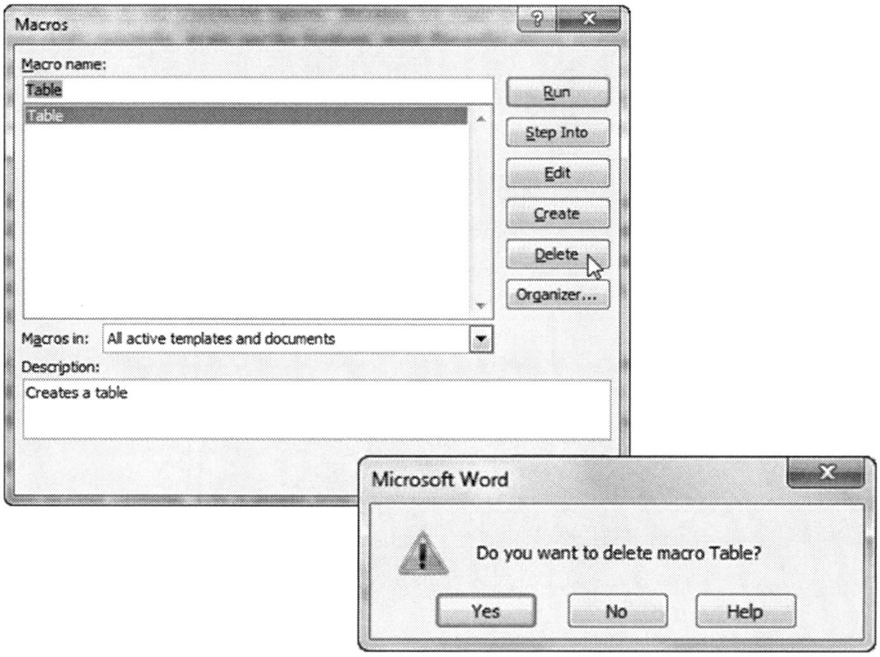

Exhibit 3-7: Deleting a macro

Do it!

B-3: Deleting a macro

Here's how	Here's why
1 Open the Macros dialog box	The Table macro is selected. You'll delete it from the My macros document.
2 Click **Delete**	To delete the macro. A message box asks for confirmation.
Click **Yes**	To delete the macro.
3 Click **Close**	To close the Macros dialog box.
4 Update and close the document	

Unit summary: Using macros

Topic A In this topic, you recorded your actions in Word to create a **macro** to automate a series of tasks. You also ran a macro. Then, you viewed a macro's code in the Microsoft Visual Basic for Applications editor.

Topic B In this topic, you edited a macro by using the **Microsoft Visual Basic for Applications editor**. You also learned how to copy and delete macros.

Independent practice activity

In this activity, you'll create a macro and copy it to another document.

The files for this activity are in Student Data folder **Unit 3\Unit summary**.

1 Open Practice macros and save it as a Word Macro-Enabled Document named **My practice macros**.

2 Create a macro called **Header** that is stored in the current document, and that shades the selected row and applies bold formatting. (*Hint:* Select the top row of the table before opening the Record Macro dialog box. Also, use the Table Tools | Design tab to apply a light shade to the selected row.)

3 Open Practice new kiosks and save it as a Word Macro-Enabled Document named **My practice new kiosks**.

4 Copy the Header macro to My practice new kiosks, as shown in Exhibit 3-8. (*Hint:* Open the Organizer dialog box from the My practice macros document.)

5 Update and close My practice macros.

6 In My practice new kiosks, select the top row of the table and run the Header macro.

7 Update and close the document.

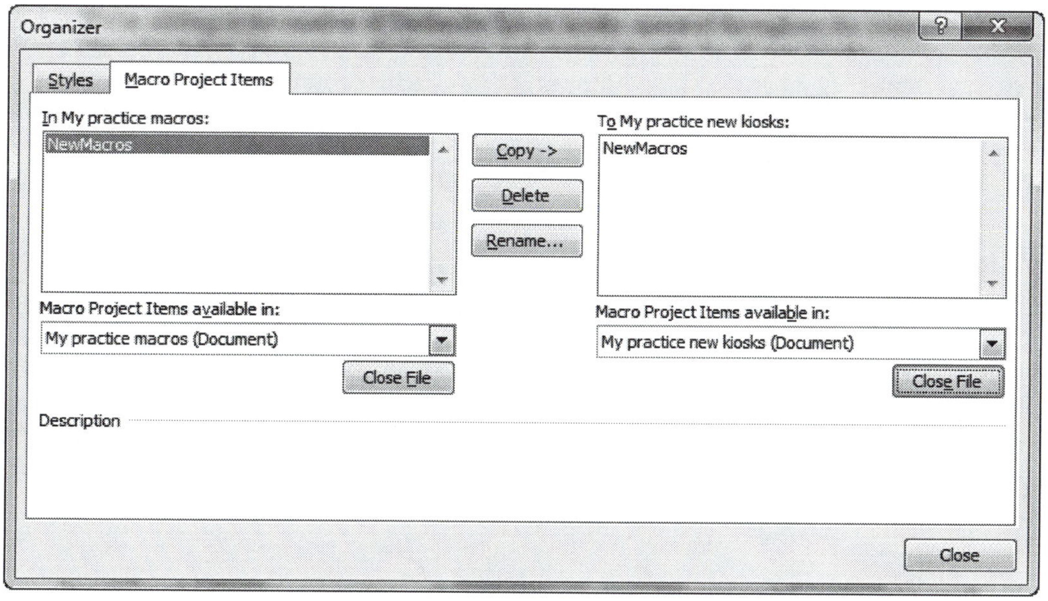

Exhibit 3-8: The Organizer dialog box as it appears in Step 4

Review questions

1 What is a macro?

2 On which tab will you find the commands for working with macros?

A Home

B Insert

C References

D View

3 How do you create a macro by recording steps you perform in Word?

A On the View tab, in the Macros group, click Macros and choose View Macro.

B On the View tab, in the Macros group, click Macros and choose Record Macro.

C On the Insert tab, in the Text group, click Quick Parts and select Field.

D On the Insert tab, in the Text group, click Object.

4 When you are finished recording the macro steps, what should you do?

5 How can you modify a macro in the Microsoft Visual Basic for Applications editor?

A In the Macros dialog box, click Edit.

B In the Macros dialog box, click Organizer.

C In the Code group, click Record Macro.

D In the Controls group, click Design Mode.

6 How can you run a macro?

7 How do you start copying a macro from one document to another?

A In the Macros dialog box, click Edit.

B In the Macros dialog box, click Organizer.

C In the Code group, click Record Macro.

D In the Code group, click Visual Basic.

Unit 4

Working with forms

Unit time: 60 minutes

Complete this unit, and you'll know how to:

A Create forms by adding labels and content controls to a Word document.

B Protect forms.

C Use the Compatibility Checker, the Document Inspector, and digital signatures to share and secure documents.

Topic A: Creating forms

This topic covers the following Microsoft Office Specialist objectives for exam 77-887: Word Expert 2010.

#	Objective
1.1	**Configure Word options**
	1.1.1 Change default program options
5.3	**Create forms**
	5.3.1 Use the Controls group
	5.3.2 Add Help content to form fields
	5.3.3 Link a form to a database
	5.3.4 Lock a form
5.4	**Manipulate forms**
	5.4.2 Add fields to a form
	5.4.3 Remove fields from a form

Types of forms

Explanation

You might want to create questionnaires or display information in a specific format. Forms help you perform these tasks. You can use Word to create three types of forms:

- Web forms are distributed on the Web. Users view and complete Web forms in a browser.
- Printed forms are completed on paper.
- Word forms are viewed and completed in Word. They can be sent to users through e-mail or posted on a network.

Form components

As shown in Exhibit 4-1, a form consists of labels and data. *Labels* describe the data being stored. For example, "Employee name" is a field label, and its corresponding data is "Jamie Morrison."

Employee information

Employee code:	42-191
Employee name:	Jamie Morrison
Address:	916 Thurmont Ave
City:	Portland
State:	OR
Zip:	97214
Department:	Marketing
Date of hire:	12/12/2006

Exhibit 4-1: A completed form

Content controls

Data is entered and stored by using *content controls,* which guide and restrict the user's actions and tell the user how to complete the form. For example, a drop-down list control provides a specific list of possible responses. Users' responses are limited to only those options in the list. Content controls also provide text to instruct users, such as "Click here to enter text," as shown in Exhibit 4-2. Content controls can be used in templates, forms, and other documents.

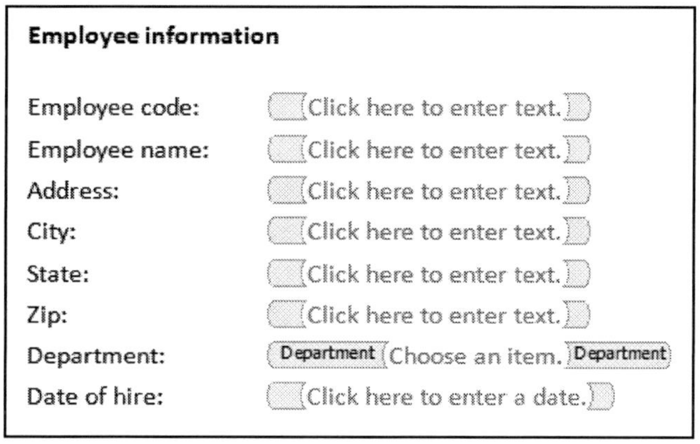

Exhibit 4-2: An uncompleted form showing content controls

Linking forms to databases

You've seen how macros can be created in Visual Basic for Applications (VBA) to automate multi-step, repetitive, or complex tasks in Word. You can also use VBA to link a Word form to a database. For example, you might want to automatically process data from submitted forms by collecting it in a database, or you might want to use information in a database to populate fields in a Word form.

Although the specifics are beyond the scope of this course, a skilled VBA programmer could use *Open Database Connectivity* (ODBC) to create those interactions between Word forms and databases. ODBC provides a set of standards by which VBA code can communicate with a wide variety of database management systems or database applications. It could be used, for example, to query a database management system, such as Microsoft SQL Server, Oracle, or MySQL, or to query a desktop database application, such as Microsoft Access or FileMaker.

Do it!

A-1: Entering data in a form

The files for this activity are in Student Data folder **Unit 4\Topic A**.

Here's how	Here's why
1 Open Sample form	
Save it as **My sample form**	In the current topic folder.
2 Observe the form	It contains a number of labels and controls.
3 Next to Employee code, click **Click here to enter text.**	
Enter **42-191**	 To add the employee code data by using a text control. Text controls are used to enter text such as names and addresses.
Press TAB	To move to the next control.
4 Enter **Jamie Morrison**	In the control for Employee name.
Press TAB	To move to the Address field.
5 Enter **916 Thurmont Ave**	
Move to the next field	Press Tab.
6 Enter the City, State, and Zip data as shown	
7 Press TAB	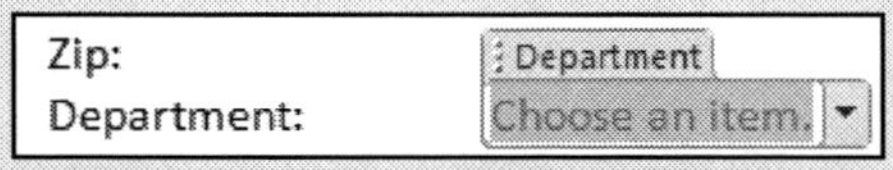 To select the Department field. A drop-down arrow appears.
Click the drop-down arrow	Because this is a drop-down list control, a list of options appears; here, it's a list of departments.
From the list, select **Marketing**	To specify this employee's department.
8 Press TAB	 To select the date field. A drop-down arrow appears.
Click the drop-down arrow	Because this is a date control, a calendar appears.
Click any date	To enter a hire date in the field.
9 Update and close the document	

Field labels

Explanation

You can begin creating a form by adding the labels that should be displayed with the content controls. You can add form labels by typing and formatting the text that you want to use for the labels.

When creating a form, you might consider creating a table to hold the form labels and fields. By using a table, you can easily align form items, and you can add formatting to improve the form's visual appearance. For example, you could add a black border to the bottom of a cell to create an underline in the printed version of the form, or you could add a color to table cells to give respondents a visual cue about the locations of the form fields.

Do it!

A-2: Adding field labels

Here's how	Here's why
1 Create a new blank document	
Save the document as **My form**	In the current topic folder.
2 Type **Employee professional development survey**	To add a heading for the survey.
Press ENTER	To move to a new paragraph.
3 Type **Employee code:**	To create the label for the text field you'll add later.
Press ENTER	
4 Add the next three labels, as shown	Employee name: Scheduled training: Start date:
Press ENTER	
5 Update the document	

Adding content controls

Explanation

The tools for adding content controls are on the Developer tab, which is not shown by default. To add the Developer tab to the Ribbon:

1 On the File tab, click Options to open the Word Options dialog box.
2 In the left pane, select Customize Ribbon.
3 In the right pane, in the Main Tabs list, check Developer. Then click OK.

On the Developer tab, you can use the tools in the Controls group, shown in Exhibit 4-3, to add content controls to your document.

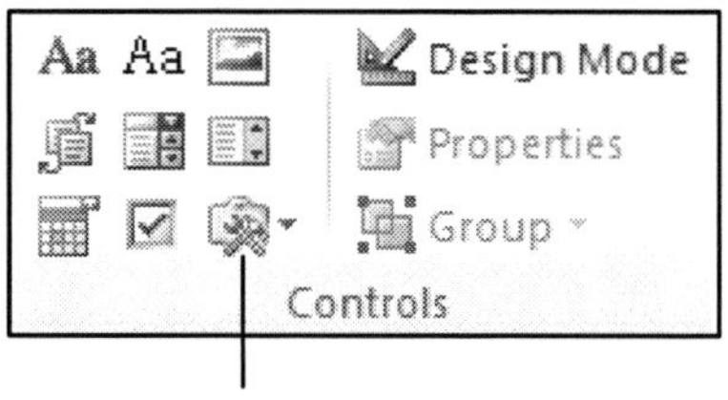

Exhibit 4-3: The Controls group on the Developer tab

To add a text control to a form:

1 Open or create the document you will use as a form.
2 Click the Developer tab.
3 In the Controls group, click Design Mode.
4 Place the insertion point where you want to add the content control.
5 Click the Plain Text content control or the Rich Text content control.

When you add a content control, it displays placeholder text, as shown in Exhibit 4-4. This text tells the form user what to do, such as "Click here to enter text."

Exhibit 4-4: Text content controls

To remove a content control from a form, click the content control to select it. Then click the handle on the left edge of the content control, as shown in Exhibit 4-5, and press Delete.

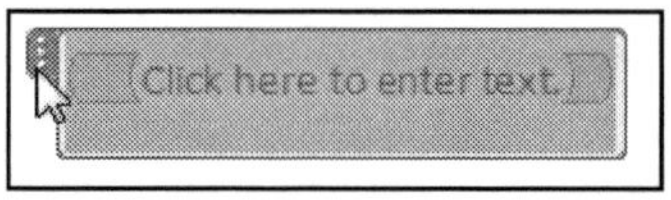

Exhibit 4-5: Removing a content control

Do it!

A-3: Adding text content controls

Here's how	Here's why
1 On the File tab, click **Options**	To open the Word Options dialog box.
2 In the left pane, click **Customize Ribbon**	To display the options for customizing the Ribbon and keyboard shortcuts.
Under Customize the Ribbon, in the Main Tabs list, check **Developer**	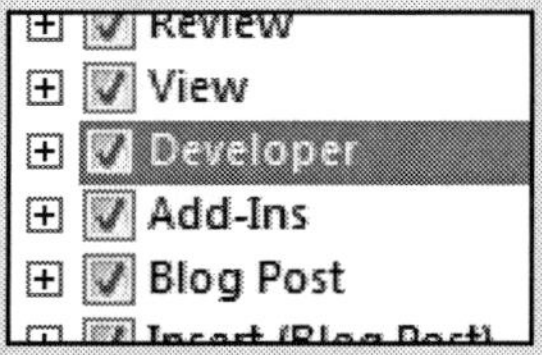
Click **OK**	The Developer tab appears after the other tabs on the Ribbon.
3 Click the **Developer** tab	You'll add a text field next to the Employee code label.
4 In the Controls group, click **Design Mode**	To view the controls in Design mode.
5 Click to the right of the "Employee code" label	
Press TAB	You're ready to insert the text content control.
6 In the Controls group, click Aa	(The Plain Text Content Control button.) To add a plain-text content control next to the "Employee code" label. The control contains placeholder text that tells the user what to do.
7 Add a plain-text content control for the "Employee name" label, as shown	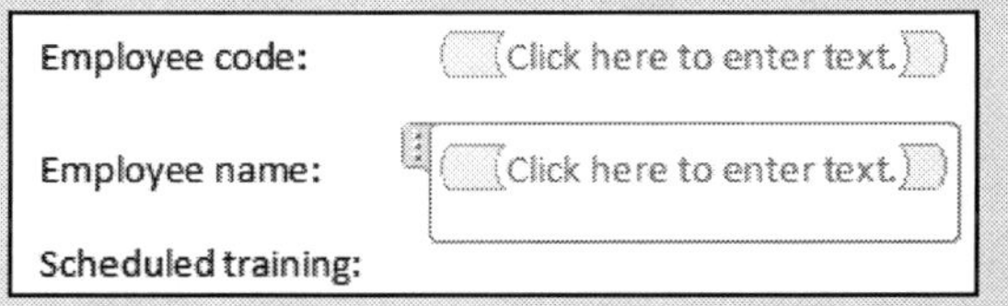 Click to the right of the label, press Tab, and click the Plain Text Content Control button in the Controls group.
8 Update the document	

Adding drop-down list controls to forms

Explanation

You use a drop-down list to provide respondents with a fixed set of values to choose from. For example, if your form contains a Company Department field, you can use a drop-down list to limit responses to only official department names. This makes completing the form easier for respondents, and it helps ensure the integrity and consistency of data. Because users can select only one option from a drop-down list, these types of form fields are available only in electronic forms (Word forms and Web forms).

To add a drop-down list control to a form:

1. In the document you will use as a form, click the Developer tab.
2. In the Controls group, click Design Mode.
3. Place the insertion point where you want to add the content control.
4. Click the Drop-Down List control.

Using the Content Control Properties dialog box

After you add a drop-down list control to a form, you'll need to populate the list with choices by using the Content Control Properties dialog box, shown in Exhibit 4-6. To open the dialog box, select the control in the document and click Properties in the Controls group. The elements of the dialog box vary depending on which control is selected.

For a drop-down list control, the Content Control Properties dialog box includes an Add button. Click Add, enter the name of the item you want to include in the list, and click OK. Continue with this procedure until your list of items is completed. Then click OK to close the Content Control Properties dialog box and save your changes.

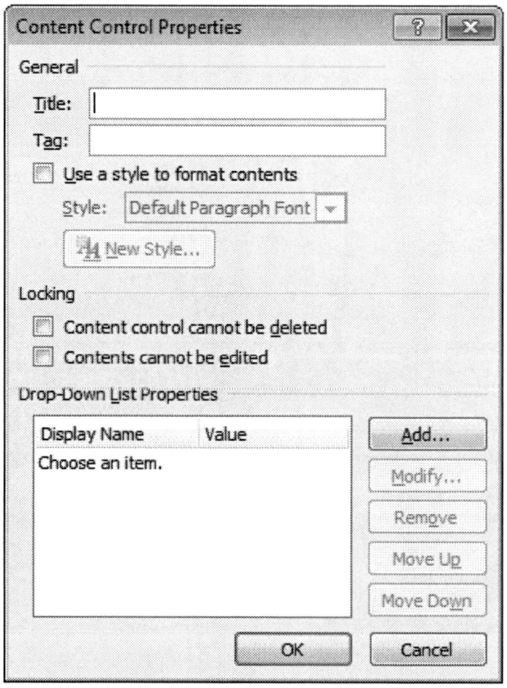

Exhibit 4-6: The properties for a drop-down list control

Protecting individual content controls

You can protect a single content control by using the Content Control Properties dialog box. Use the options under Locking to protect the selected control. For a drop-down list, you can protect the control from being deleted and protect the list from being edited.

Do it!

A-4: Adding a drop-down list to a form

Here's how	Here's why
1 Click to the right of the "Scheduled training" label	
Press TAB	To align the insertion point with the previous controls.
2 In the Controls group, click 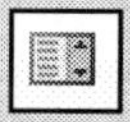	(The Drop-Down List control.) To add a drop-down list control next to the "Department" label.
3 In the Controls group, click **Properties**	To open the Content Control Properties dialog box.
4 In the Title box, enter **Training**	To give the control a name.
5 Click **Add**	To open the Add Choice dialog box. You enter options for the drop-down list here.
In the Display Name box, enter **Conferences or seminars**	To specify a category of training to be included in the drop-down list.
Click **OK**	To add the name to the list.
6 Add a category called **Online training** to the list	Click Add, enter "Online training" in the Display Name box, and click OK.
7 Add a category called **College-level classes** to the list	Notice that "College-level classes" is added to the bottom of the current list. You want to arrange this list in alphabetical order.
8 Under Display Name, select **College-level classes**	In the Content Control Properties dialog box.
Click **Move Up**	To move the list item up one place in the order.
Click **Move Up**	To move the list item up one more place in the order. Now the list is in alphabetical order.
9 Click **OK**	To accept the drop-down list properties and close the dialog box.
Update the document	

Adding date content controls to forms

Explanation

If you want users to enter a date in your form, you can add the Date Picker content control. When a user selects this control, a drop-down arrow appears. Clicking the arrow displays an interactive calendar, which can be used to navigate to the desired date.

To add a date content control to a form:

1. Place the insertion point where you want to add the control.
2. Click the Developer tab.
3. In the Controls group, click the Date Picker control button.

You can modify the properties of this control by selecting it in the document and clicking the Properties button in the Controls group.

Do it!

A-5: Adding a date control

Here's how	Here's why
1 Click to the right of the "Start date" label	
Press TAB twice	To align the insertion point with the previous controls.
2 In the Controls group, click 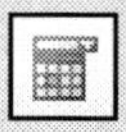	(The Date Picker control.) To add a date field to the form.
3 In the Controls group, click **Properties**	To open the Content Control Properties dialog box. The options in this dialog box change depending on the content control selected.
4 Under Date Picker Properties, verify that the **M/d/yyyy** format is selected	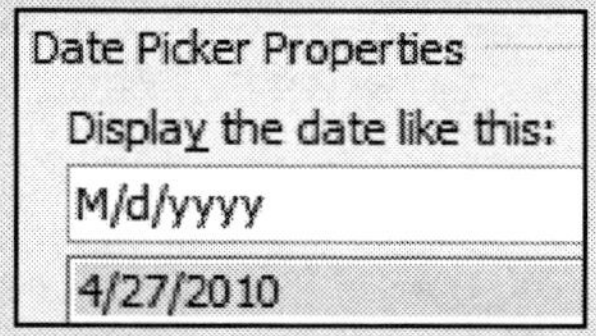 To specify this date format for the field.
Click **OK**	To close the dialog box, accepting the default properties. The settings will become apparent when a respondent fills out the form.
5 In the Controls group, click **Design Mode**	To exit Design mode.
Update the document	

Legacy tools

Explanation

Word groups additional form fields in the Legacy Tools section of the Controls group. To view and insert these fields, click the Legacy Tools button, shown in Exhibit 4-3, and click the desired field. To remove a field, select it and press Delete.

Some of the fields on your form might accept data only if it's entered in a specific format. A first-time form user might not know the format in which the data needs to be entered. To provide some help, you can add help text to fields. This specific help text is known as *context-sensitive help*.

To add context-sensitive help text to a field:

1 Select the field.
2 In the Controls group on the Developer tab, click Properties.
3 Click Add Help Text to open the Form Field Help Text dialog box, shown in Exhibit 4-7.
4 Click the tab that controls where the help text is displayed.
  - Use the Status Bar tab to display help text on the status bar when the form field is selected.
  - Use the Help Key (F1) tab to display help text in a separate window after users press F1.
5 Select "Type your own" and enter a message in the box. (Or you can use an AutoText entry.)
6 Click OK.

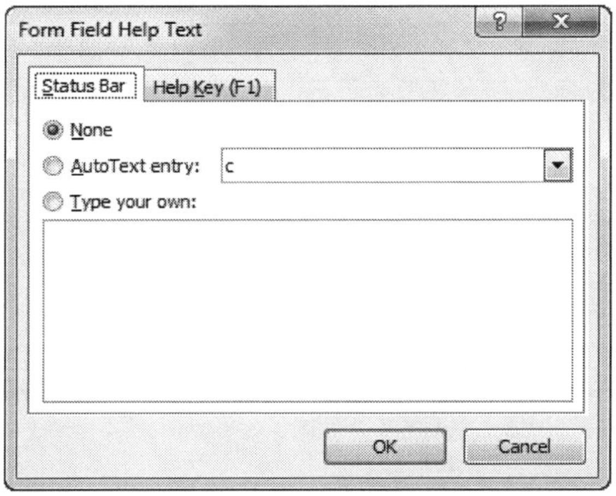

Exhibit 4-7: The Form Field Help Text dialog box

Do it!

A-6: Adding check box fields

Here's how	Here's why
1 Place the insertion point at the end of the document	On the line below "Start date."
Type **Select your preferred contact method**	
Press ENTER	
2 In the Controls group, click	(The Legacy Tools button.) To display Legacy Forms fields and ActiveX Controls.
Click	The Check Box Form Field button. (Legacy forms)
3 Press SPACEBAR	
Type **Email**	
Press ENTER	
4 Add check box fields and labels as shown	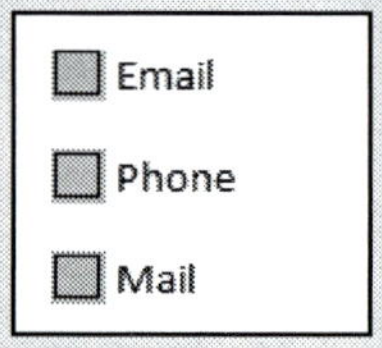
5 Double-click the **Email** check box	To open the Check Box Form Field Options dialog box.
6 Click **Add Help Text**	To open the Form Field Help Text dialog box. By default, the Status Bar tab is active. You'll add help text to the Email field.
Select **Type your own**	
In the box, enter the help message shown	
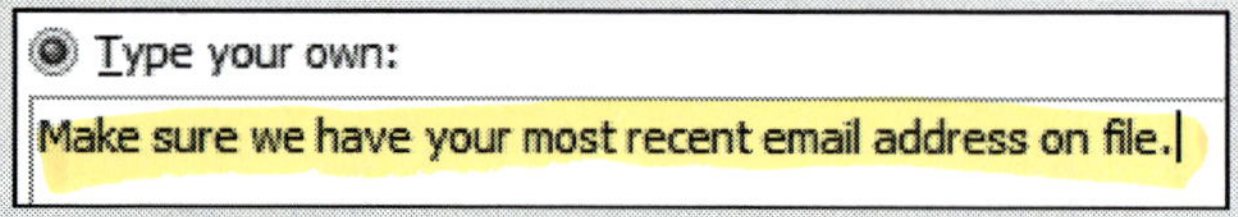	
Click **OK**	To close the dialog box.
7 Click **OK**	To close the Check Box Form Field Options dialog box.
Update and close the document	

Topic B: Protecting forms

This topic covers the following Microsoft Office Specialist objectives for exam 77-881: Word 2010.

#	Objective
1.2	**Apply protection to a document**
	1.2.2 Applying protection by using the Ribbon commands

This topic covers the following Microsoft Office Specialist objectives for exam 77-887: Word Expert 2010.

#	Objective
1.2	**Apply protection to a document**
	1.2.2 Apply controls or restrictions to document access
5.3	**Create forms**
	5.3.4 Lock a form
5.4	**Manipulate forms**
	5.4.1 Unlock a form

Preventing unwanted changes

Explanation

You can protect a form from unwanted changes by assigning a password to it. When you protect a document, you can specify which parts of it can be modified by selected users. Use the Restrict Formatting and Editing task pane, shown in Exhibit 4-8, to protect a document with a password and to specify sections that can be modified by selected users.

To protect a form by using the Restrict Formatting and Editing pane:

1. On the Review tab, click Restrict Editing to open the Restrict Formatting and Editing pane.
2. Under Editing restrictions, check "Allow only this type of editing in the document." Then select "Filling in forms."
3. Under Start enforcement, click Yes, Start Enforcing Protection to open the Start Enforcing Protection dialog box.
4. In the "Enter new password (optional)" box, type a password. Type the same password in the "Reenter password to confirm" box.
5. Click OK.

Note: Passwords are case-sensitive. Also, you must remember your password because forgotten ones cannot be retrieved.

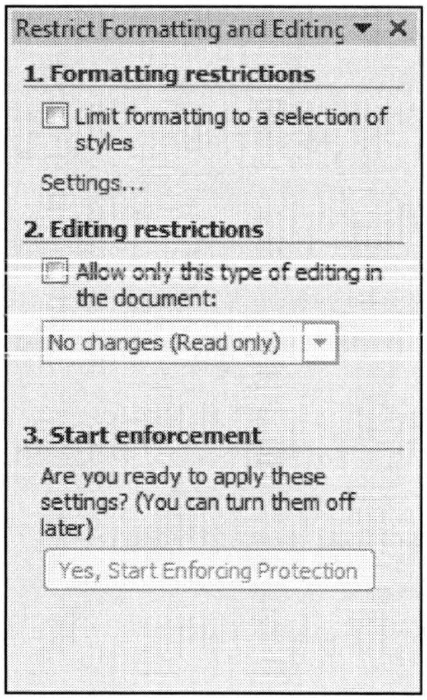

Exhibit 4-8: The Restrict Formatting and Editing pane

Do it!

B-1: Protecting a form

The files for this activity are in Student Data folder **Unit 4\Topic B**.

Here's how	Here's why
1 Open New form and save it as **My new form**	
Click the **Review** tab	
In the Protect group, click **Restrict Editing**	To open the Restrict Formatting and Editing pane. You'll protect the form so that unauthorized users cannot change it.
2 Under Editing restrictions, check **Allow only this type of editing in the document**	
3 From the list under Editing restrictions, select **Filling in forms**	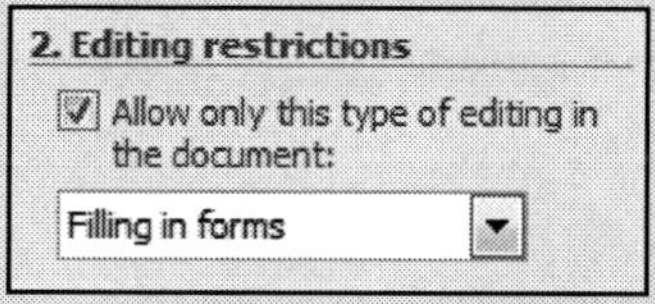 To specify that users can fill in the form, but can make no other types of changes in the file.
4 Click **Yes, Start Enforcing Protection**	To open the Start Enforcing Protection dialog box.
5 In the "Enter new password (optional)" box, enter **password**	To specify a password for the form. (123456)
In the "Reenter password to confirm" box, enter **password**	To confirm the password.
Click **OK**	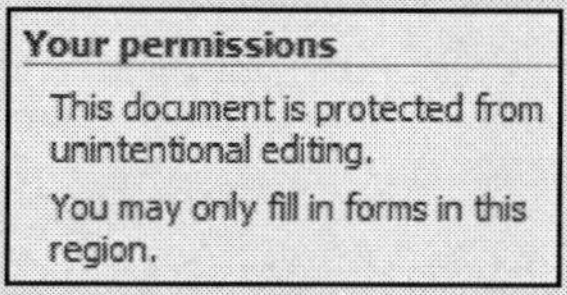 The Restrict Formatting and Editing pane displays a message stating that the document is protected with a password and you can only fill in the form.
6 Fill out the form	(The specific data you enter is not important.) Because the form is protected, you can enter form data but can't make any other kinds of changes. To make other types of changes, you'd have to use a password to unprotect the document.
7 Update the document	

Unprotecting forms

Explanation

You need to unprotect a form before you can modify it. To unprotect a password-protected document:

1. In the Restrict Formatting and Editing pane, click Stop Protection to open the Unprotect Document dialog box.
2. In the Password box, enter the password.
3. Click OK.

Do it!

B-2: Removing protection

Here's how	Here's why
1 Click **Stop Protection**	(At the bottom of the Restrict Formatting and Editing pane.) To open the Unprotect Document dialog box.
2 In the Password box, enter **password**	This is the password you assigned to protect the form.
3 Click **OK**	To close the Unprotect Document dialog box and unprotect the form.
4 Update the document	

Setting editing permissions

Explanation

If you protect a form by using a password, you will need to unprotect the form each time you want to modify it. To avoid this, you can specify the users who can modify the form even while protection is turned on.

To add a user with special permissions:

1. Open the form.
2. Open the Restrict Formatting and Editing pane.
3. Under Editing restrictions, check "Allow only this type of editing in the document."
4. Under Exceptions (optional), click More users to open the Add Users dialog box, shown in Exhibit 4-9.
5. Specify the names of the users by entering their Microsoft Windows user account names or their e-mail addresses.
6. Click OK. The users' names appear, along with check boxes, in the Restrict Formatting and Editing pane.
7. Under Start enforcement, click Yes, Start Enforcing Protection. Then specify the password and click OK.

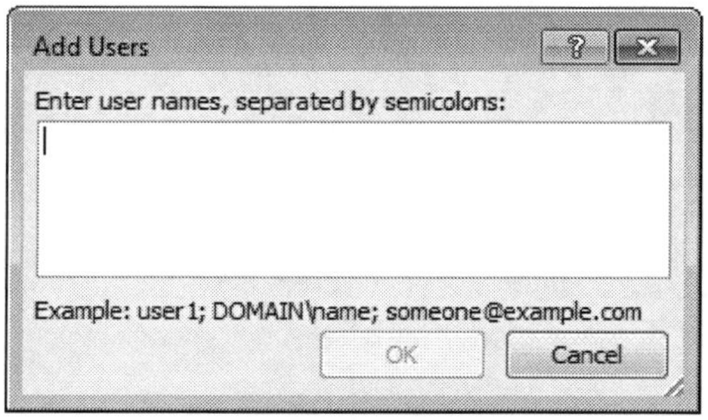

Exhibit 4-9: The Add Users dialog box

After adding a user, you can specify the part of the form that he or she can modify. To do so, select the part of the form that you want to be editable, and check the box next to the user name in the Restrict Formatting and Editing pane.

Do it!

B-3: Setting permissions for a user

Here's how	Here's why
1 Under Editing restrictions, from the list, select **No changes (Read only)**	(In the Restrict Formatting and Editing pane.) To specify that when the document is protected, no changes will be permitted.
2 Under Exceptions (optional), click **More users...**	To open the Add Users dialog box.
3 Observe the dialog box	You can identify specific users who will be granted exceptions to any editing restrictions.
Click **Cancel**	To close the Add Users dialog box. Any users identified in this dialog box would appear, along with check boxes, under Exceptions in the Restrict Formatting and Editing pane.
4 Select the last two lines of the form	(The "Scheduled training" and "Start date" labels and controls.) To specify the part of the document that will be editable for the specified users.
Under Exceptions (optional), check **Everyone**	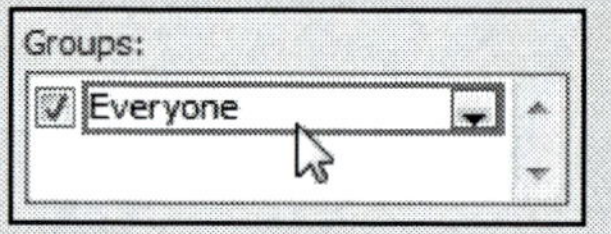
5 Click **Yes, Start Enforcing Protection**	To open the Start Enforcing Protection dialog box.
6 In the "Enter new password (optional)" box, enter **password**	All users except those specified under exceptions will be required to enter a password if they have to change the form.
In the "Reenter password to confirm" box, enter **password**	To confirm the password.
Click **OK**	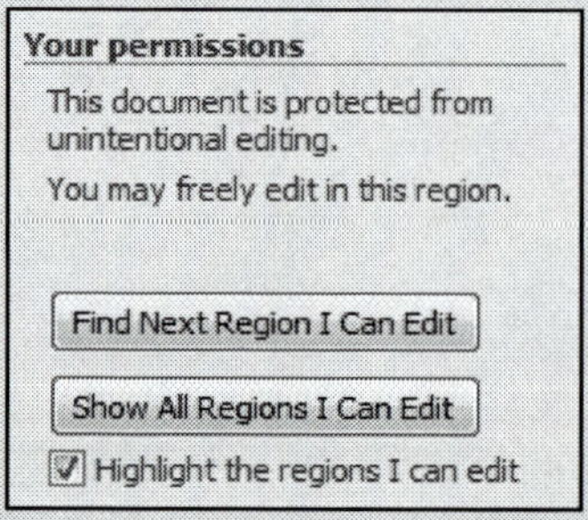 The document is protected with a password; however, special restrictions are in effect. The areas you can edit will be highlighted.

7	Press CTRL + HOME	To deselect the text. The portion of the document that can be edited is highlighted in yellow.
	Click **Find Next Region I Can Edit**	(In the Restrict Formatting and Editing pane.) To move to the region you can modify.
8	Click **Stop Protection**	To open the Unprotect Document dialog box.
	Enter the password	Type "password" in the box.
	Click **OK**	To close the dialog box and unprotect the form. The document is still highlighted, which indicates that the permissions are still set. You need to clear the check box near your user name to remove the permissions.
9	Select the last two lines of the form	(If necessary.) The "Scheduled training" and "Start date" labels and controls.
	Clear **Everyone**	To remove the permissions.
10	Press END	To deselect the text. Nothing in the document is highlighted.
	Close the Restrict Formatting and Editing pane	
11	Update and close the document	

Topic C: Sharing and securing documents

This topic covers the following Microsoft Office Specialist objectives for exam 77-881: Word 2010.

#	Objective
1.2	**Apply protection to a document**
	1.2.1 Apply protection by using the Microsoft Office Backstage view commands
	1.2.1.3 Mark as Final
1.4	**Share documents**
	1.4.5 Create PDF documents
	1.4.6 Create

Finalizing documents

Explanation

When a document is complete, you can use a series of features to finalize it before sharing it with others. Click the File tab and click Info to display the Info page, which contains options for setting permissions, sharing the file, managing version control, and modifying properties.

The Compatibility Checker

If you're sharing your documents with other people who are using previous versions of Word, you'll want to check for elements that aren't supported or that behave differently in these other versions. These elements can include building blocks, citations, bibliographies, content controls, embedded objects, SmartArt graphics, and tracked changes that involve moving text. To check for unsupported elements, use the Compatibility Checker.

To run the Compatibility Checker:

1. On the File tab, click Info.
2. On the Info page, click the Check for Issues button and choose Check Compatibility.
3. Select the versions you want to show: either Word 97-2003 or Word 2007. Both options are selected by default.

Incompatibilities are identified and listed for your review. If you save a document in the Word 97-2003 file format, the Compatibility Checker will run automatically. To save a file in this format, click the File tab and click Save As. In the Save as type list, select Word 97-2003 Document. Click Save.

Do it!

C-1: Using the Compatibility Checker

The files for this activity are in Student Data folder **Unit 4\Topic C**.

Here's how	Here's why
1 Open New form2	
2 Open the Save As dialog box	
From the Save as type list, select **Word 97-2003 Document**	To save the file in the .doc file format, which is used in Word versions 97–2003.
Click **Save**	The Compatibility Checker runs automatically, opening the Microsoft Office Word Compatibility Checker dialog box.
3 Observe the message	The content controls in this form aren't compatible with the Word 97-2003 file format. To make this document compatible, Word will convert the content controls to static text.
Click **Continue**	To accept this alteration and continue saving the document in the Word 97-2003 format.
4 Observe the title bar	Word is now operating in Compatibility mode.
5 Place the insertion point at the end of the document	After the date.
Press ENTER	
6 Enter **Years employed:**	To add another label.
Press TAB	To align the insertion point with the previous controls.
7 Click the **Developer** tab	
In the Controls group, click **Design Mode**	
Observe the buttons in the Controls group	The content controls are not available because they're not compatible with the Word 97-2003 format. Only compatible operations can be performed.
8 Close the document without saving	

The Document Inspector

Explanation

The *Document Inspector* checks for hidden metadata, like comments, and for personal information that you might not want other readers to see. To open the Document Inspector, click the File tab and click Info. On the Info page, click the Check for Issues button and choose Inspect Document. Click Inspect to start the evaluation.

The Document Inspector checks the following elements:

- Comments, revisions, and annotations
- Document properties and personal information
- Custom XML data
- Headers, footers, and watermarks
- Hidden text

Finalizing a document

To finalize a document, display the Info page, click the Protect Document button, and choose Mark as Final. By marking a document as Final, you indicate that editing is completed, and the file is then read-only. Word disables typing, editing commands, and proofing marks. The status property is set to Final, and the Mark As Final icon is displayed in the status bar. (To make the document editable again, repeat the steps you used to mark it as final.)

Do it!

C-2: Using the Document Inspector

The files for this activity are in Student Data folder **Unit 4\Topic C**.

Here's how	Here's why
1 Open Edited	
Save the document as **My edited**	In the current topic folder.
2 Observe the deleted text	The text is marked as deleted with a strikethrough, and new text is underlined next to it.
3 Click the **File** tab	Info should be selected on the File tab.
View the document properties	(On the right side of the Info page.) The document's author and title are identified.
4 On the Info page, click **Check for Issues** and choose **Inspect Document**	To open the Document Inspector dialog box.
5 Observe the categories	These are the document elements that will be inspected. You can clear any element that you don't want to include in the inspection.
6 Click **Inspect**	The Document Inspector reviews the contents.
Observe the results	The Document Inspector identifies the revision marks and document properties as elements that you might want to remove before sharing this document.

7	For Comments, Revisions, Versions, and Annotations, click **Remove All**	To remove revision marks so that other people will not see the changes that have been made.
8	For Document Properties and Personal Information, click **Remove All**	To remove the author name and title. You don't want others to see the names of people who worked on the document.
9	Click **Close**	To return to the document.
	Observe the document and its properties	There are no more revision marks, and properties have been cleared.
10	Click the **File** tab	The Info page should be displayed.
	Click **Protect Document** and choose **Mark as Final**	A message box appears, stating that this will mark the document as final and make it read-only.
11	Click **OK**	To finalize the document. Another message box appears, explaining that because this file is now final, it can no longer be edited.
	Click **OK** and return to the Home tab	
12	Observe the Information bar across the top of the document	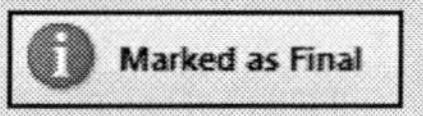 It tells you that the file has been marked as final, to discourage editing, and gives you the option to edit it anyway.
	Observe the icon on the left side of the status bar	 (The Marked as Final icon.) This indicates that the document has been saved and finalized.

Publishing documents in the PDF and XPS file formats

Explanation

If you're creating a document to be shared with other users, consider that some members of your intended audience might not have Word 2010 or Word 2007. If they don't, they might not be able to open a document saved in the .docx file format. For documents that will primarily be read and printed, such as résumés or newsletters, you can save them in a fixed-layout format. This type of file format preserves a document's appearance and makes it easier to share files with people who don't have Word.

Two fixed-layout electronic file formats are PDF and XPS. PDF stands for Portable Document Format; Adobe Systems developed this format and released the first version of it in 1992. PDF documents can be read in Adobe Reader, which can be downloaded for free from Adobe's Web site. XPS stands for XML Paper Specification; this format was developed by Microsoft. The XPS Viewer comes with Windows Vista and Windows 7 and is available for Windows XP and Windows Server 2003.

The PDF and XPS formats preserve a document's formatting and ensure that the document's data cannot easily be changed. These formats are useful for viewing a document online or in print. The PDF format is also useful for documents that will be printed using commercial printing methods.

To save a document in the PDF or XPS file format:

1. With the document open in Word 2010, open the Save As dialog box.
2. Enter a name for the file.
3. From the Save as type list, select either PDF or XPS Document.
4. Click Save.

Do it!

C-3: Publishing a file as an XPS document

Here's how	Here's why
1 Click the **File** tab	
2 Click **Save As**	
3 In the File name box, enter **My publication**	
From the Save as type list, select **XPS Document**	To specify the file format to be used.
Verify that **Open file after publishing** is checked	
Click **Save**	To save the document and open it in the XPS Viewer. This viewer enables other users to read and print the document, independently of Word.
4 Scroll through the document	The document's formatting has been preserved.
5 Close the viewer	Click the Close button in the upper-right corner of the window.
Close the Word document	Don't save changes.

Digital signatures

Explanation

A *digital signature* is an electronic security stamp that is used to authenticate a form, macro, or document. The signature helps you confirm that the file, macro, or e-mail message originated from the person who signed it and that no one has altered it. To use a digital signature, you need to obtain and install a digital certificate. A *digital certificate* is a file that verifies that a digital signature is valid.

To obtain a digital certificate, you or your organization should submit an application to a commercial certification authority, such as VeriSign Inc. The application can also be submitted to your internal security administrator or an information technology (IT) professional. You can also create your own digital certificates, called *self-signed projects*, by using the Selfcert.exe tool. However, self-signed projects might be considered unauthenticated and might generate a warning because they aren't sanctioned by any certification authority.

When you receive a digital certificate, you also receive instructions on how to install it on your computer. After installing the certificate, you can use it as a digital signature to sign a file. After a document is signed digitally, it becomes read-only. This prevents modifications and preserves the integrity of the document.

Do it!

C-4: Discussing digital signatures

Questions and answers

1 What is a digital signature?

2 Why would you use a digital signature?

3 What is a digital certificate?

4 What is the risk of creating your own digital certificate?

5 True or false? After a document is digitally signed, it becomes read-only.

Unit summary: Working with forms

Topic A In this topic, you created a form by adding **labels** to it. You also added text, drop-down list, and date controls. Next, you modified **control properties**.

Topic B In this topic, you protected a form by using the **Restrict Formatting and Editing pane**. You also learned how to set **permissions** for a user to modify specified regions of a protected form.

Topic C In this topic, you used the **Compatibility Checker** and the **Document Inspector** to prepare a document for sharing with others. You also published a document in the **XPS** file format. Finally, you discussed **digital signatures**. You learned that you must install a digital certificate to use a digital signature.

Independent practice activity

In this activity, you'll create a form and enter data into it.

The files for this activity are in Student Data folder **Unit 4\Unit summary**.

1 Open Practice form and save it as **My practice form**. This document contains several labels in the left column of a table. You'll add field content controls in the right column of the table.

2 Enter text fields in the table cells next to the following labels: Employee code, Employee name, Address, City, State, and Zip.

3 Enter a date field in the cell next to the "Date of birth" label. Format the field as a date with the format MMMM d, yyyy. (*Hint:* Use the Date Picker control.)

4 Protect the form so that all modifications are prohibited, except for filling in forms. For the protection password, enter **password**. (*Hint:* In the Restrict Formatting and Editing pane, under Editing restrictions, select **Filling in forms**. You'll need to turn off Design Mode to enforce protection.)

5 Update the document.

6 Enter the data shown in Exhibit 4-10. (*Hint:* You can enter the date by typing it. You don't have to use the calendar tool.)

7 Close the Restrict Formatting and Editing pane.

8 Update and close the form.

Employee information

Employee code:	46-971
Employee name:	Jesse Bennett
Address:	3150 Simmons Ct
City:	Portland
State:	OR
Zip:	97217
Date of birth:	October 30, 1980

Exhibit 4-10: The form data after Step 6

Review questions

1 What three types of forms can you create in Word?

2 Which tab contains controls used to create form fields?

A Insert

B Page Layout

C Developer

D Design

3 How can you open the Properties dialog box for a form field?

4 If you want to protect a form by specifying a password, what should you do?

A In the Controls group, click Lock.

B In the Controls group, click Properties.

C Use the options in the Restrict Formatting and Editing pane.

D Click Legacy Tools and click the Reset Form Fields button.

5 If you want to locate hidden metadata, like comments and personal information that you might not want other readers to see, what tool can you use?

A The Find command

B The Compatibility Checker

C The Restrict Formatting and Editing pane

D The Document Inspector

6 What is the difference between a digital signature and a digital certificate?

Unit 5
Customizing Word

Unit time: 60 minutes

Complete this unit, and you'll know how to:

A Customize the Ribbon by adding tabs and groups, and minimize the Ribbon.

B Customize the Quick Access toolbar.

C Create keyboard shortcuts.

Topic A: Customizing the Ribbon

This topic covers the following Microsoft Office Specialist objectives for exam 77-887: Word Expert 2010.

#	Objective
1.1	**Configure Word options**
	1.1.1 Change default program options

Options for changing the Ribbon

Explanation

You can customize the Ribbon by adding your own tabs and groups and by rearranging the tabs. You can also minimize the Ribbon to get more screen space.

Minimizing the Ribbon

The Ribbon puts commonly used commands within easy reach, but it takes up a lot of space on the screen. Some users prefer to minimize the Ribbon, as shown in Exhibit 5-1, in order to have more screen space while they're working. You can minimize the Ribbon either by clicking the Minimize the Ribbon button or by double-clicking the active tab. The Minimize the Ribbon button is the caret-shaped button to the left of the Help button, at the right end of the Ribbon.

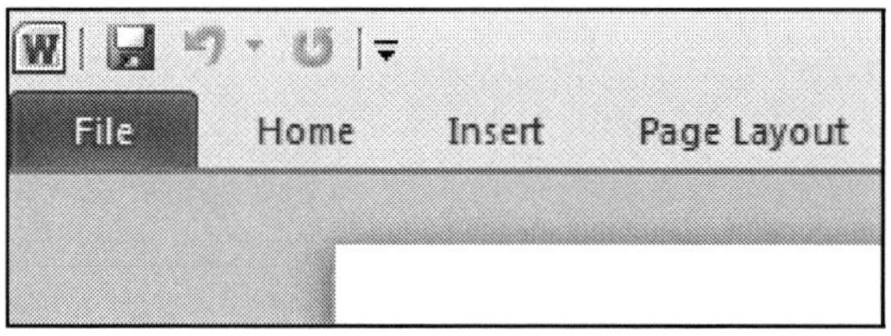

Exhibit 5-1: The Ribbon can be minimized to save screen space

Once you have minimized the Ribbon, you can click a tab to temporarily show it so you can access a command. The Ribbon will be displayed until you click a command or click elsewhere in the window. Then it will be hidden again.

To expand the Ribbon and keep it expanded, click the Expand the Ribbon button (the down-pointing caret) or double-click a tab.

Do it!

A-1: Hiding and showing the Ribbon

Here's how	Here's why
1 At the right end of the Ribbon, click 	To minimize the Ribbon, giving you more space to work in your documents.
2 Click 	To expand the Ribbon.
3 Double-click the **Home** tab	The Ribbon is minimized.
4 Click the **Home** tab	To temporarily expand the Ribbon.
Click in the document area	The Ribbon is automatically minimized again.
5 Double-click the **Home** tab	To expand the Ribbon.
Click in the document area	The Ribbon stays expanded now.

Customizing the Ribbon

Explanation

A new feature in Word 2010 is the ability to customize the Ribbon. You can add tabs and groups and then add commands to them, and you can change the order of the tabs.

To customize the Ribbon, click the File tab, click Options, and click Customize Ribbon. You can also right-click any tab and choose Customize the Ribbon. Either method opens the Customize the Ribbon page of the Word Options dialog box, shown in Exhibit 5-2. The tabs and groups, as well as the commands they contain, are listed in the list box on the right.

Rearranging tabs, groups, and commands

To rearrange items, select an item in the Customize the Ribbon list box and click the Move Up or Move Down buttons. For example, to move the Review tab to the left of (before) the Mailings tab, select Review and click the Move Up button (the up-pointing triangle).

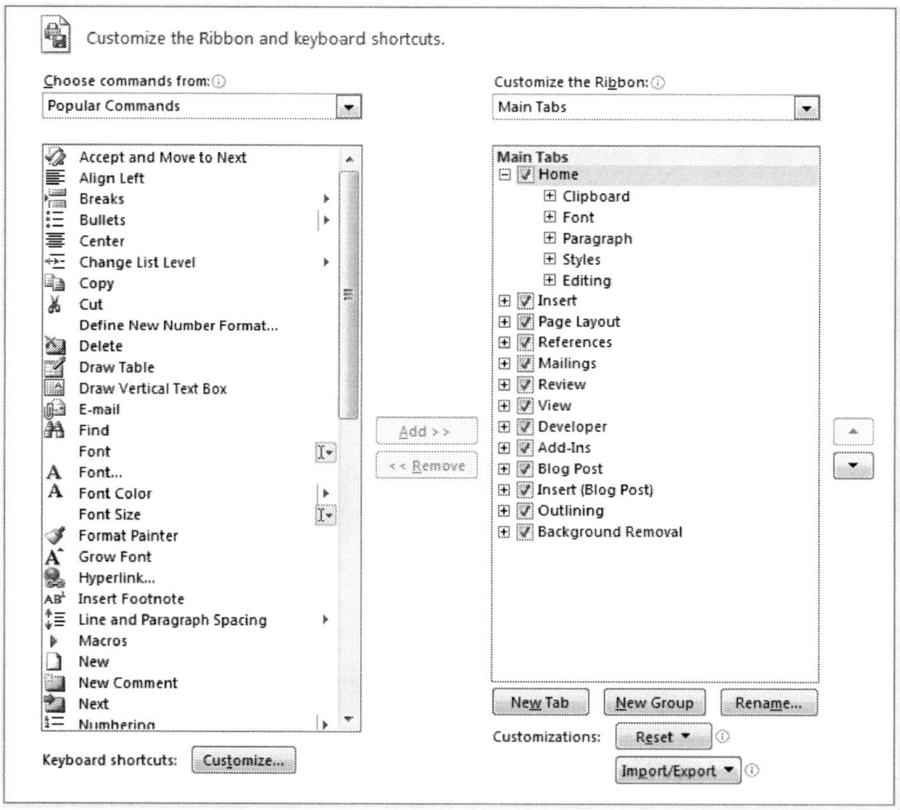

Exhibit 5-2: Customizing the Ribbon

Do it!

A-2: Rearranging Ribbon tabs

Here's how	Here's why
1 Observe the order of the tabs on the Ribbon	By default, the tabs are, from left to right, File, Home, Insert, Page Layout, References, Mailings, Review, and View.
2 Click the **File** tab and click **Options**	To open the Word Options dialog box.
In the left pane, click **Customize Ribbon**	
3 In the Customize the Ribbon list box, select **Mailings** and then click the Move Up button, as shown	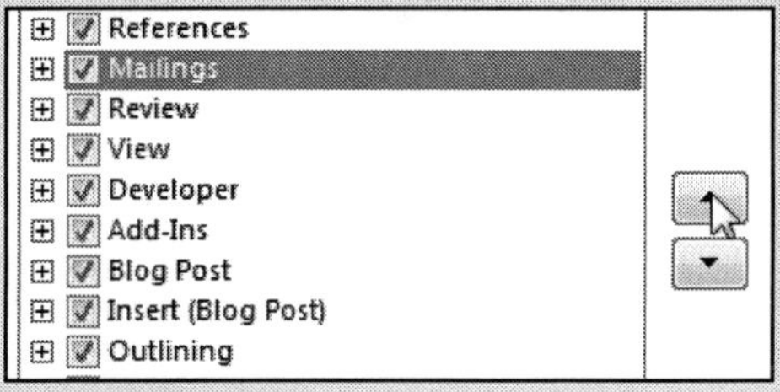 To move the Mailings tab up and thus to the left of the References tab.
4 Click **OK**	The tabs are arranged in the new order you specified.
5 On the Home tab, observe the order of command groups	By default, from left to right, the groups are Clipboard, Font, Paragraph, Styles, and Editing.
6 Right-click the **Home** tab and choose **Customize the Ribbon…**	To open the Word Options dialog box, with the Customize the Ribbon page active.
7 Under Home, select **Paragraph**	
Click 	(The Move Up button.) To move the Paragraph group before the Font group.
8 Click **OK**	The groups have been rearranged.

Hiding and removing tab elements

Explanation

You can remove entire groups of commands from a tab. However, you cannot remove individual commands from the built-in groups. Likewise, you cannot remove built-in tabs, but you can hide them.

To hide a tab, open the Customize the Ribbon page of the Word Options dialog box and clear the tab's check box. To remove a command group, select it and click Remove. If you have created a custom tab of your own, you can remove it in the same way: select it and click Remove.

Do it!

A-3: Hiding and removing tabs and groups

Here's how	Here's why
1 Right-click the **Home** tab and choose **Customize the Ribbon…**	
2 Clear **Insert**	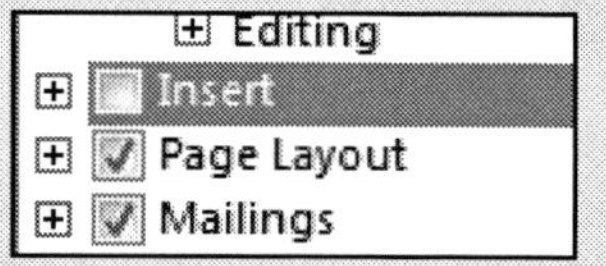 To hide the Insert tab.
3 Under Home, select **Editing**	
Click **Remove**	To remove this command group from the Home tab.
4 Click **OK**	The Insert tab is no longer visible, and the Editing group on the Home tab is gone.

Custom tabs and groups

Explanation

You can create your own tabs and command groups. You might do so to put the commands you use most often within easy reach. To create a tab:

1. Open the Customize the Ribbon page of the Word Options dialog box.
2. Click the New Tab button. The new tab appears in the Customize the Ribbon list box and contains a new group. Both the tab and the group have a default name, which you can change.
3. To rename the tab, select it and click Rename. Type the new name and click OK.
4. To rename the default group, select it and click Rename. Type the new name and click OK.

You can add groups by clicking New Group, and you can rearrange them by using the Move Up and Move Down buttons.

To add a command to a group, select the group. Then, from the "Choose commands from" list, select a category of commands. Select the desired command in the left-hand list box and click Add.

Do it!

A-4: Creating a tab

Here's how	Here's why
1 Right-click the **Home** tab and choose **Customize the Ribbon...**	
2 Click **New Tab**	Your new tab is created after the Home tab. It has a default name and contains a single, default group named New Group (Custom).
3 Select **New Tab (Custom)**	
Click **Rename**	
Type **Favorites** and click **OK**	To rename your tab.
4 Select **New Group (Custom)** and click **Rename**	
Type **Word Commands** and click **OK**	To rename the default group.
5 From the "Choose commands from" list, select **All Commands**	
6 Scroll down the list and select **Normal Word Document**	
Click **Add**	To add the Normal Word Document command to your Word Commands group.
7 Add **Copy**, **Paste**, and **Undo** to your group	Select each command and click Add.
8 In the right-hand list box, in your Word Commands group, select **Undo**	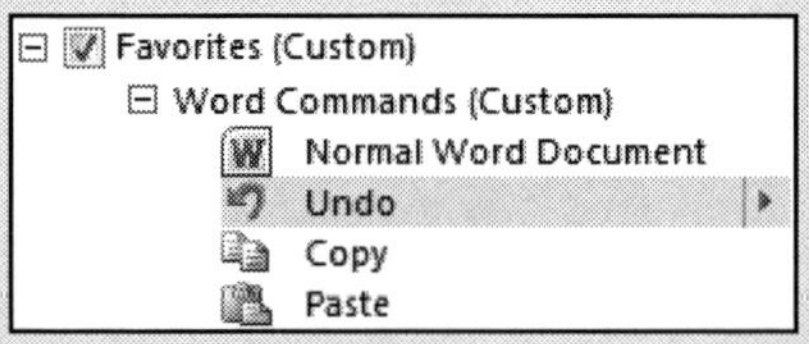
Click [▲] twice	To move Undo ahead of Copy in the list of commands.
9 In the right-hand list box, select **Favorites (Custom)**	
Click [▲]	To move your tab so it's first in the list.
10 Click **OK**	The Favorites tab is listed after File and before Home.
Click the **Favorites** tab	It contains the commands you specified.

Resetting the Ribbon

Explanation

You can reset the Ribbon to its default configuration, either tab by tab or in its entirety. For example, let's say you modified the Home and View tabs. You could reset one of those tabs to its default state while leaving the other customized, or you could remove all customizations.

To reset the Ribbon, open the Customize the Ribbon page of the Word Options dialog box. Then, to reset a single tab, select it, click Reset, and select "Reset only selected Ribbon tab." To reset all customizations, click Reset, select "Reset all customizations," and click Yes. Click OK to close the dialog box.

Note that the "Reset all customizations" option also resets the Quick Access toolbar if it has been changed.

Do it!

A-5: Resetting the Ribbon

Here's how	Here's why
1 Right-click the **Favorites** tab and choose **Customize the Ribbon...**	
2 Click **Reset**	
Choose **Reset all customizations**	A warning box appears, asking whether you want to delete all Ribbon and Quick Access toolbar customizations.
Click **Yes**	To reset the Ribbon to its default state.
3 Click **OK**	To close the Word Options dialog box.

Topic B: Customizing the Quick Access toolbar

This topic covers the following Microsoft Office Specialist objectives for exam 77-887: Word Expert 2010.

#	Objective
1.1	**Configure Word options**
	1.1.1 Change default program options
5.2	**Apply and manipulate macro options**
	5.2.4 Create a custom macro button on the Quick Access Toolbar

Adding buttons to the toolbar

Explanation

By default, the Quick Access toolbar contains only three buttons: Save, Undo, and Redo. You can customize the Quick Access toolbar to include buttons for additional commands and tools. Because the Quick Access toolbar is always visible, you'll be able to click buttons for your most frequently used commands, regardless of which Ribbon tab is active.

To add buttons to the Quick Access toolbar, click the arrow on the right side of the toolbar. The Customize Quick Access Toolbar menu is displayed. From this menu, you can choose from many commonly used commands, such as New, Open, and Quick Print.

If the menu does not contain the command you want to add, you can still add it to the toolbar. Here's how:

1. From the Customize Quick Access Toolbar menu, choose More Commands to open the Word Options dialog box with the Quick Access Toolbar options displayed.
2. From the "Choose commands from" list, select a category of commands.
3. In the list of commands, select the command you want to add to the Quick Access toolbar.
4. Click Add to move the selected command to the right-hand list box, as shown in Exhibit 5-3.
5. Click OK.

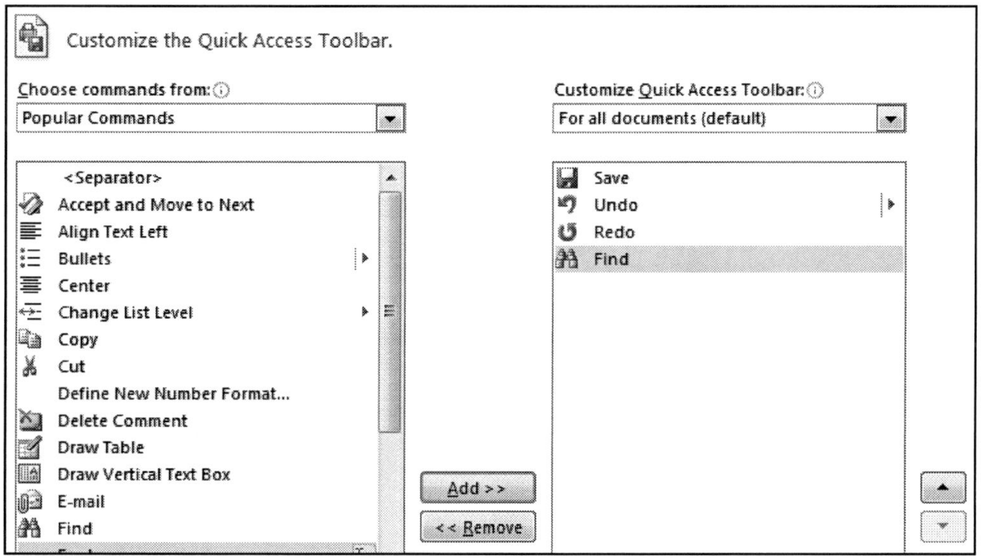

Exhibit 5-3: Adding commands to the Quick Access toolbar

Do it!

B-1: Adding buttons to the Quick Access toolbar

The files for this activity are in Student Data folder **Unit 5\Topic B**.

Here's how	Here's why
1 Open Custom	
Save the document as **My custom**	You'll add several commands to the Quick Access toolbar.
2 Click as shown	 To display the Customize Quick Access Toolbar menu.
Choose **New**	To add a button for the New command to the Quick Access toolbar. This button will create a new document.
3 Display the Customize Quick Access Toolbar menu	On the right side of the Quick Access toolbar, click the arrow.
Choose **Open**	To add a button for the Open command to the toolbar. This button will open the Open dialog box.
4 Display the Customize Quick Access Toolbar menu (Right click)	
Choose **More commands...**	To open the Word Options dialog box with the Quick Access Toolbar options displayed. You'll add the Close command to the Quick Access toolbar.
5 From the "Choose commands from" list, select **File Tab**	To display the commands listed on the File tab.
In the list of commands, select **Close**	Use the list box on the left side of the dialog box.
Click **Add**	To move the selected command to the right-hand list box. By default, this list represents the toolbar that is available for all Word documents. You could also select the current document's name from the Customize Quick Access Toolbar list to customize the toolbar for the current document only. Next, you'll add several commands for working with table layouts.
6 From the "Choose commands from" list, select **Table Tools | Layout Tab**	To display all of the table layout commands.

7	Add the following commands to the toolbar: **Insert Rows Above** **Insert Rows Below** **Merge Cells**	Select each command in the left-hand list box and click Add.
	Click **OK**	The new buttons appear on the Quick Access toolbar. Next, you'll merge two of the cells in the table.
8	Select the top-right two cells, as shown	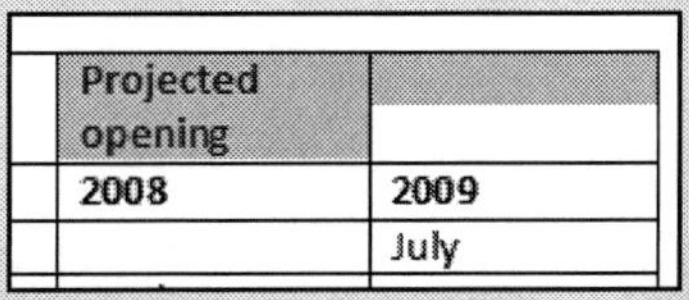
	On the Quick Access toolbar, click	(The Merge Cells button.) To merge the cells. Because you added this button to the Quick Access toolbar, you can use it any time, regardless of which Ribbon tab is active.
9	Update the document	
10	On the Quick Access toolbar, click	(The Close button.) To close the document.

Changing toolbar display options

Explanation

After adding buttons to the Quick Access toolbar, you might want to change their arrangement. In addition, if you add a lot of buttons, you might want to move the toolbar below the Ribbon so that the buttons can extend across the window without crowding the tabs.

To rearrange the Quick Access toolbar buttons:

1. Open the Word Options dialog box with the Quick Access Toolbar options displayed.
2. In the right-hand list of commands, select a command you want to move, and click Move Up or Move Down as necessary.
3. Click OK.

To move the Quick Access toolbar below the Ribbon, click the arrow on the right side of the toolbar and choose Show Below the Ribbon. You can return the toolbar to its default location by clicking the arrow and choosing Show Above the Ribbon. You can also specify the Quick Access toolbar position by checking or clearing "Show Quick Access Toolbar below the Ribbon" in the Word Options dialog box.

Do it!

B-2: Customizing the Quick Access toolbar display

Here's how	Here's why
1 Open the Word Options dialog box, with the Quick Access Toolbar options displayed	Click the arrow on the right side of the Quick Access toolbar and choose More Commands.
2 In the right-hand list box, select **New**	
3 Click [▲] three times	(The Move Up button.) To move the New command up in the list.
4 Move the **Open** command to just below the New command	Select Open and click Move Up.
5 Check **Show Quick Access Toolbar below the Ribbon**	In the bottom-left corner of the dialog box.
6 Click **OK**	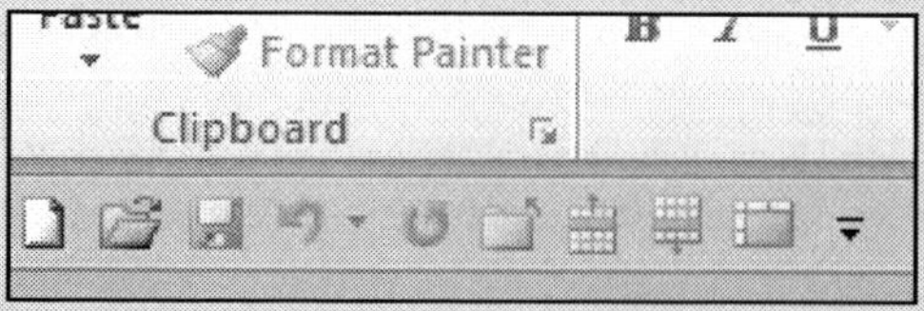 The Quick Access toolbar now appears below the Ribbon, and the buttons are in the order you specified.

Adding macros to the toolbar

Explanation

After creating a macro, you can add a button for it to the Quick Access toolbar. To do this:

1. Open the Word Options dialog box with the Quick Access Toolbar options displayed.
2. From the "Choose commands from" list, select Macros to display the available macros.
3. In the list of macros, select the one you want, and click Add to move it to the right-hand list box.
4. Click OK.

Do it!

B-3: Adding a macro to the Quick Access toolbar

Here's how	Here's why
1 On the Quick Access toolbar, click [Open button]	(The Open button.) The Open dialog box appears.
2 Open My custom	This file contains a macro that you'll add to the Quick Access toolbar.
3 Open the Word Options dialog box, with the Quick Access Toolbar options displayed	
4 From the "Choose commands from" list, select **Macros**	The Project.NewMacros.Table macro appears in the list.
5 In the list of macros, select **Project.NewMacros.Table**	
Click **Add**	To add the macro to the toolbar.
Click **OK**	
6 Move the insertion point to the end of the document	(Press Ctrl+End.) You'll use the Project.NewMacros.Table macro button to insert a table.
Press ↵ ENTER	
7 On the Quick Access toolbar, click [macro button]	(The Project.NewMacros.Table button.) To run the Table macro.
8 Update the document	

Removing buttons from the toolbar

Explanation

You can remove any buttons from the Quick Access toolbar, including the three default buttons. To remove a button from the Quick Access toolbar:

1 Open the Word Options dialog box with the Quick Access Toolbar options displayed.
2 In the right-hand list box, select the item you want to remove from the toolbar.
3 Click Remove and then click OK.

You can also remove a button by right-clicking it and choosing "Remove from Quick Access Toolbar." To return the Quick Access toolbar to its default buttons, open the Word Options dialog box to the Quick Access Toolbar page, click Reset, and click OK.

Do it!

B-4: Resetting the Quick Access toolbar

Here's how	Here's why
1 Open the Word Options dialog box, with the Quick Access Toolbar options displayed	You'll remove the macro you added to the Quick Access toolbar.
2 In the right-hand list box, select **Project.NewMacros.Table**	
Click **Remove**	To remove the Project.NewMacros.Table macro button from the toolbar.
	You'll return the toolbar to its default buttons.
3 Click **Reset** and choose **Reset only Quick Access Toolbar**	A message asks you to verify that you want to return the toolbar to its default state.
Click **Yes**	To remove all but the default toolbar buttons.
4 Clear **Show Quick Access Toolbar below the Ribbon**	To return the Quick Access toolbar to its default location.
Click **OK**	The Quick Access toolbar appears in its default location, with the default buttons.
5 Close the document	Don't save changes.

Topic C: Customizing keyboard shortcuts

This topic covers the following Microsoft Office Specialist objectives for exam 77-887: Word Expert 2010.

#	Objective
1.1	**Configure Word options**
	1.1.1 Change default program options

Creating a keyboard shortcut

Explanation

Many of Word's most commonly used commands have keyboard shortcuts. For example, to italicize selected text, you can press Ctrl+I rather than click the Italics button on the Home tab. However, many commands do not have an associated keyboard shortcut. You can assign a keyboard shortcut to any command in Word.

Home (Right click) Customize the ribbon

To add a keyboard shortcut:

1. Open the Word Options dialog box and select Customize Ribbon.
2. Next to Keyboard shortcuts, click Customize to open the Customize Keyboard dialog box, shown in Exhibit 5-4.
3. In the Categories list, select a category.
4. In the Commands list, select the command to which you want to assign a shortcut key.
5. Place the insertion point in the "Press new shortcut key box" and press the shortcut keys you want to assign. Under the Current keys box, the "Currently assigned to" text indicates whether the shortcut is already in use.
6. Click Assign to assign the shortcut, which then appears in the Current keys list.
7. Click Close to close the Customize Keyboard dialog box.
8. Click OK to close the Word Options dialog box.

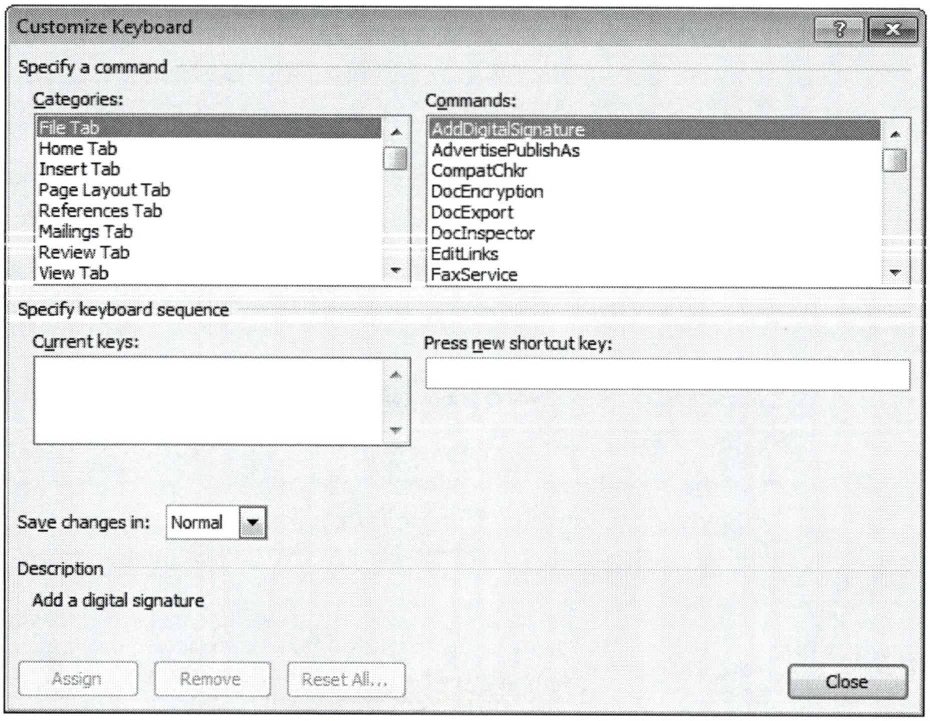

Exhibit 5-4: The Customize Keyboard dialog box

Do it!

C-1: Adding keyboard shortcuts

The files for this activity are in Student Data folder **Unit 5\Topic C**.

<table>
<tr><th>Here's how</th><th>Here's why</th></tr>
<tr><td>1 Open the Word Options dialog box

In the left pane, select Customize Ribbon</td><td>You'll create a keyboard shortcut for a table layout commands.</td></tr>
<tr><td>2 Next to Keyboard shortcuts, click Customize</td><td>(At the bottom of the dialog box.) To open the Customize Keyboard dialog box.</td></tr>
<tr><td>3 In the Categories list, select Table Tools | Layout Tab</td><td>
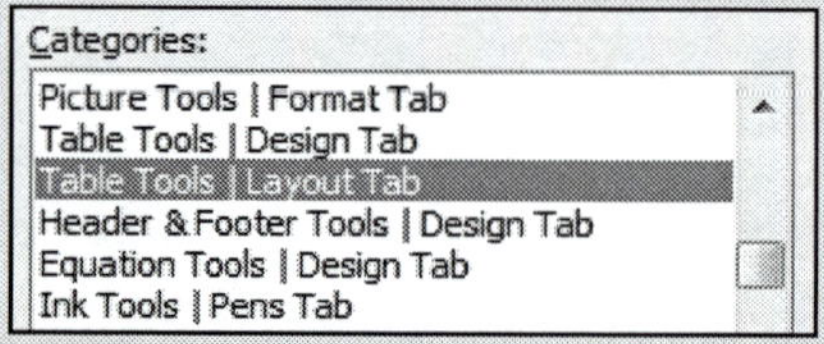

To display all of the commands in the Table Tools | Layout category.</td></tr>
<tr><td>4 In the Commands list, select TableInsertRowAbove</td><td>
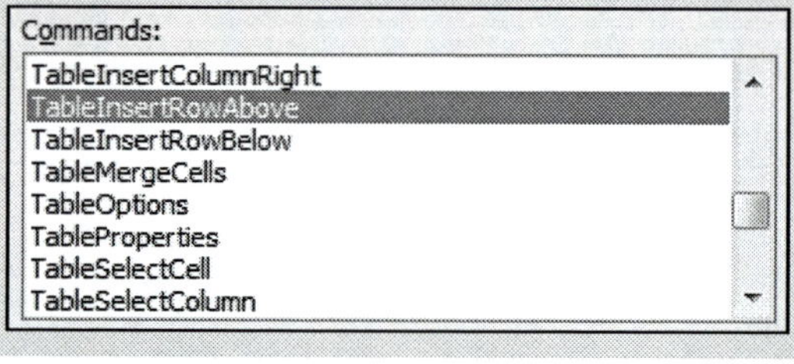

</td></tr>
</table>

5	Place the insertion point as shown	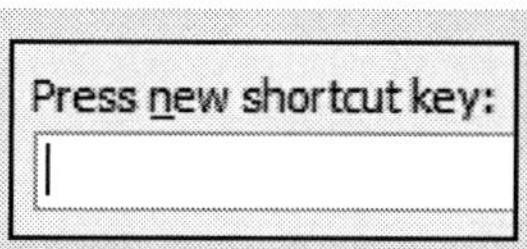 You'll assign a shortcut key to TableInsertRowAbove.
	Press CTRL + I	
	Observe the text below the Current keys box	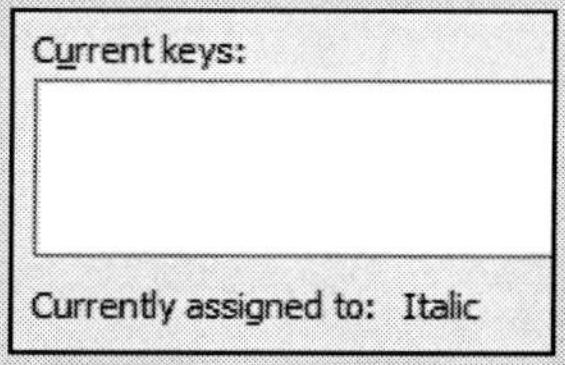 This shortcut is already assigned to the Italic command. You'll leave that shortcut with its current command and try another shortcut.
6	Press ← BACKSPACE	To delete the shortcut.
	Press CTRL + ALT + SHIFT + I	To try another shortcut. This one is unassigned.
7	Click **Assign**	 To add the shortcut to the Current keys box.
	Click **Close**	To close the Customize Keyboard dialog box.
8	Click **OK**	To close the Word Options dialog box.
9	Open Custom2 and save it as **My custom file2**	You'll use the shortcut to add a new row above "Albany, NY."
10	Click in the table row containing "Albany, NY"	You might need to scroll.
	Press CTRL + ALT + SHIFT + I	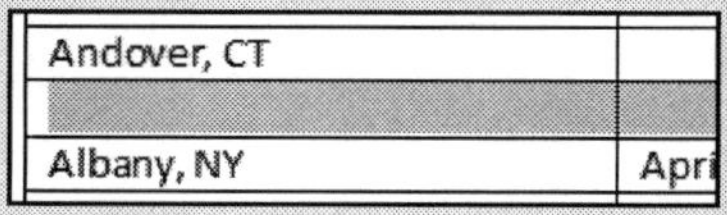 To insert a new row above the current row.

Returning to the default keyboard shortcuts

Explanation

You might want to return to the default keyboard shortcuts, removing any new shortcuts you've assigned. To do so:

1. Open the Word Options dialog box and display the Customize Ribbon options.
2. Next to Keyboard shortcuts, click Customize to open the Customize Keyboard dialog box.
3. Click Reset All.
4. Click Yes to verify that you want to reset keyboard shortcuts.
5. Click Close to return to the Word Options dialog box, and then click OK.

Do it!

C-2: Resetting keyboard shortcuts

Here's how	Here's why
1 Open the Word Options dialog box	
Verify that the Customize the Ribbon page is displayed	
2 Next to Keyboard shortcuts, click **Customize**	To open the Customize Keyboard dialog box.
3 Click **Reset All**	A message box appears, warning you that this action will remove all keys currently assigned to macros and styles in the Normal template.
Click **Yes**	To reset all keyboard shortcuts.
4 Click **Close**	To return to the Word Options dialog box.
5 Click **OK**	To close the Word Options dialog box.
6 Update and close all documents	

Unit summary: Customizing Word

Topic A In this topic, you learned how to show and hide the Ribbon and how to **customize the Ribbon** by rearranging tabs, hiding tabs and commands, and removing groups. You also learned how to add your own custom tabs and groups, and add commands to them.

Topic B In this topic, you customized the **Quick Access toolbar** by adding, rearranging, and removing buttons. You also reset the Quick Access toolbar to its default buttons.

Topic C In this topic, you assigned custom **keyboard shortcuts** to Word commands. You also reset all keyboard shortcuts to the Word defaults.

Independent practice activity

In this activity, you'll customize the Quick Access toolbar and assign new keyboard shortcuts to several commands.

The files for this activity are in Student Data folder **Unit 5\Unit summary**.

1 Open Practice customizing and save it as **My practice customizing**.

2 Add a button for the Print Preview and Print command to the Quick Access toolbar.

3 Set the Quick Access toolbar to be displayed below the Ribbon.

4 Compare the Quick Access toolbar to Exhibit 5-5.

5 Click the Print Preview button; then click the Home tab.

6 Return the Quick Access toolbar to its default buttons and its default location.

7 Update and close the file.

8 Assign the keyboard shortcut Ctrl+Alt+Shift+D to the InsertDateTime command. (*Hint:* It's in the Insert Tab category.)

9 Create a new blank file to test the keyboard shortcut.

10 Press Ctrl+Alt+Shift+D. The Date and Time dialog box appears.

11 Click OK to insert the date.

12 Reset all keyboard shortcuts to their defaults.

13 Close the file without saving it.

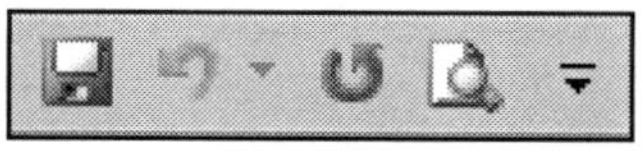

Exhibit 5-5: The Quick Access toolbar after Step 4

Review questions

1 Name two ways to hide the tabs on the Ribbon.

2 What is the procedure for creating a custom tab?

3 Can you delete built-in tabs?

4 Describe the procedure for resetting all Ribbon customizations.

5 How can you add buttons to the Quick Access toolbar? [Choose all that apply.]

A Drag items from the Ribbon to the Quick Access toolbar.

B Right-click any Ribbon item and choose Add to Quick Access Toolbar.

C Click the arrow on the Quick Access toolbar and choose More Commands.

D On the Developer tab, in the Controls group, click Insert and choose Toolbar Button.

6 How can you rearrange the Quick Access toolbar buttons?

A Point to a button and drag it along the toolbar.

B In the Word Options dialog box, select an item in the list of toolbar buttons and click Move Up or Move Down.

C Press Ctrl and drag a button along the toolbar.

D Right-click the toolbar, choose Customize Quick Access Toolbar, drag the buttons in the dialog box that appears, and click OK.

7 How can you move the Quick Access toolbar below the Ribbon?

A In the Word Options dialog box, check "Show Quick Access Toolbar below the Ribbon."

B Point to the left edge of the toolbar and drag it below the Ribbon.

C Open the Word Options dialog box, drag the toolbar to move it, and click OK.

D Press Ctrl, point to the left edge of the toolbar, and drag it below the Ribbon.

8 How can you remove a button from the Quick Access toolbar?

A With the Word Options dialog box open, drag a button away from the toolbar.

B Drag a button to the Recycle Bin icon.

C Press Ctrl and drag a button away from the toolbar.

D In the Word Options dialog box, select an item in the list of toolbar buttons and click Remove.

9 How can you open the Customize Keyboard dialog box?

A In the Word Options dialog box, display the Customize Ribbon options and click Customize.

B Right-click a button on any Ribbon tab and choose Customize Quick Access Toolbar.

C On the Developer tab, in the Controls group, click Design.

D Click the arrow on the Quick Access toolbar and choose Customize Shortcuts.

Unit 6
Long documents

Unit time: 90 minutes

Complete this unit, and you'll know how to:

A Create a master document and add a cover page.

B Create, modify, and update a table of contents and a table of figures.

C Create an index, a bibliography, a table of authorities, and footnotes.

D Work with bookmarks and cross-references.

E Add frames to a Web page document.

Topic A: Master documents

This topic covers the following Microsoft Office Specialist objectives for exam 77-881: Word 2010.

#	Objective
1.1.	**Apply different views to a document**
	1.1.4 Arrange document views
	1.1.4.2 Master documents
	1.1.4.3 Subdocuments
3.3	**Construct content in a document by using the Quick Parts tool**
	3.3.1 Add built-in building blocks
	3.3.1.5 Cover page

Master documents and subdocuments

Explanation

A *master document* is a document in which you insert a collection of other documents. Each of these inserted documents is called a *subdocument*. It's useful to store subdocuments in a master document when you want to combine multiple documents to form a single document, such as combining chapters to form a book. You can edit each subdocument separately.

Inserting subdocuments

You can add subdocuments to a master document by using the Outlining tab, which appears when you use Outline view. Subdocuments can be edited and formatted in the same way as any other document.

To insert a subdocument:

1. Create a document that will become the master document.
2. In the status bar, click the Outline button to switch to Outline view. The Outlining tab, shown in Exhibit 6-1, appears on the Ribbon.
3. In the Master Document group, click Show Document. Additional buttons, including Create and Insert, appear in that group.
4. In the Master Document group, click Insert to open the Insert Subdocument dialog box.
5. Select the file that you want to insert as a subdocument, and click Open.

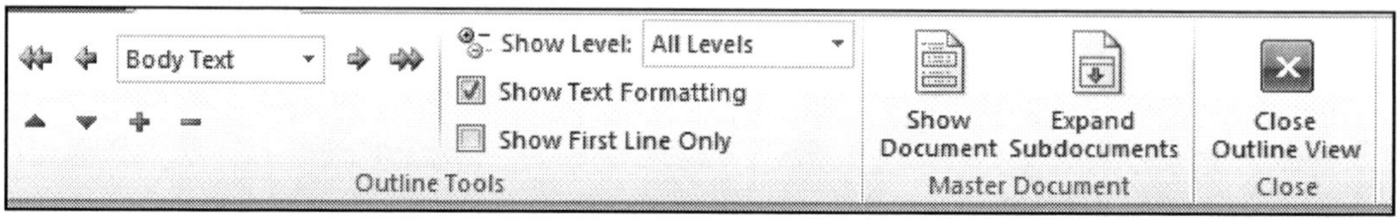

Exhibit 6-1: The Outlining tab

Do it!

A-1: Inserting subdocuments

The files for this activity are in Student Data folder **Unit 6\Topic A**.

Here's how	Here's why
1 Create a new blank document	You'll create a master document by inserting subdocuments.
Save the document as **My master**	In Student Data folder Unit 6\Topic A.
2 In the status bar, click the Outline button	 To switch to Outline view. The Outlining tab appears on the Ribbon.
3 Verify that the Outlining tab is active	
4 In the Master Document group, click **Show Document**	 Additional buttons, including Create and Insert, appear in the group.
Click **Insert**	(In the Master Document group.) To open the Insert Subdocument dialog box.
5 Navigate to the current topic folder	(Student Data folder Unit 6\Topic A.) If necessary.
Select **Chapter 1**	If this file doesn't appear in the list, select All Files or All Word Documents from the Files of type list.
Click **Open**	A message box is displayed, stating that the Heading 2 style exists in both documents.
Click **No to All**	The styles in both documents have the same formatting, so you don't need to rename any styles. The Chapter 1 file is added to the current document as a subdocument.
6 Verify that the insertion point is at the end of the document	You'll insert another subdocument here.
7 Open the Insert Subdocument dialog box	In the Master Document group, click Insert.
8 Insert **Chapter 2** as a subdocument	From the list of Files, select Chapter 2, and click Open.
Click **No to All**	

9	Insert **Chapter 3** as a subdocument	You don't need to rename any styles.
	Insert **Kiosks** as a subdocument	You don't need to rename any styles. The master document now contains four subdocuments: Chapter 1, Chapter 2, Chapter 3, and Kiosks.
10	Update the document	

Master Document view

Explanation

Master Document view is similar to Outline view. However, in Master Document view, the Subdocument icon appears in the upper-left margin of each subdocument, as shown in Exhibit 6-2. You can select the entire subdocument by clicking this Subdocument icon. To display the document in Master Document view, click Show Document in the Master Document group on the Outlining tab.

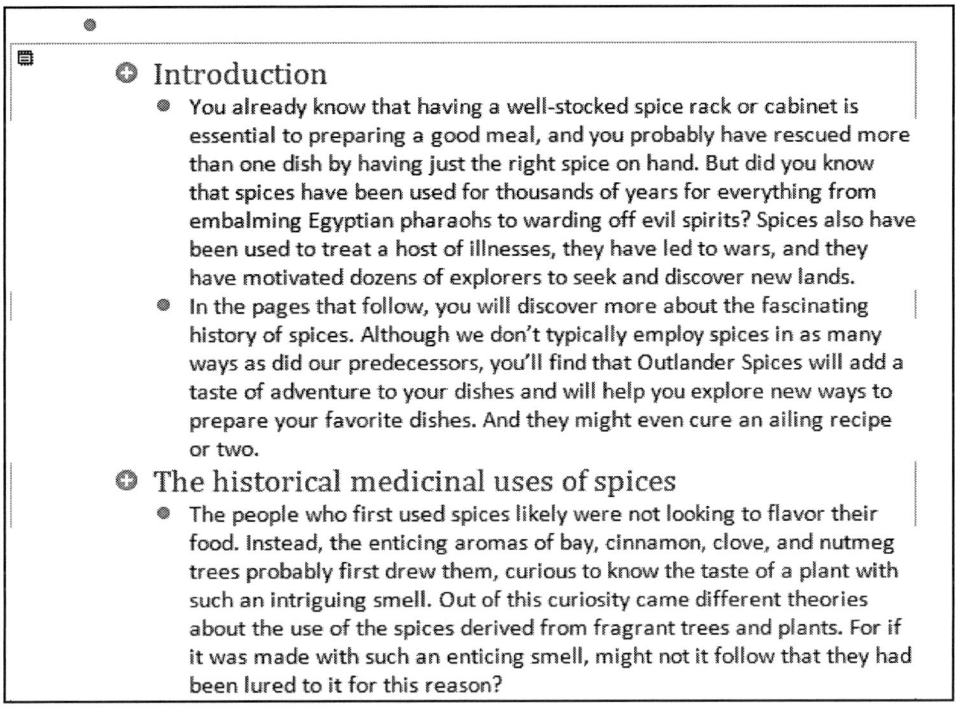
Introduction

- You already know that having a well-stocked spice rack or cabinet is essential to preparing a good meal, and you probably have rescued more than one dish by having just the right spice on hand. But did you know that spices have been used for thousands of years for everything from embalming Egyptian pharaohs to warding off evil spirits? Spices also have been used to treat a host of illnesses, they have led to wars, and they have motivated dozens of explorers to seek and discover new lands.
- In the pages that follow, you will discover more about the fascinating history of spices. Although we don't typically employ spices in as many ways as did our predecessors, you'll find that Outlander Spices will add a taste of adventure to your dishes and will help you explore new ways to prepare your favorite dishes. And they might even cure an ailing recipe or two.

The historical medicinal uses of spices

- The people who first used spices likely were not looking to flavor their food. Instead, the enticing aromas of bay, cinnamon, clove, and nutmeg trees probably first drew them, curious to know the taste of a plant with such an intriguing smell. Out of this curiosity came different theories about the use of the spices derived from fragrant trees and plants. For if it was made with such an enticing smell, might not it follow that they had been lured to it for this reason?

Exhibit 6-2: Master Document view

You can expand and collapse the text under the headings by clicking the plus and minus signs, respectively. When the subdocuments are collapsed, hyperlinks to the files appear, as shown in Exhibit 6-3.

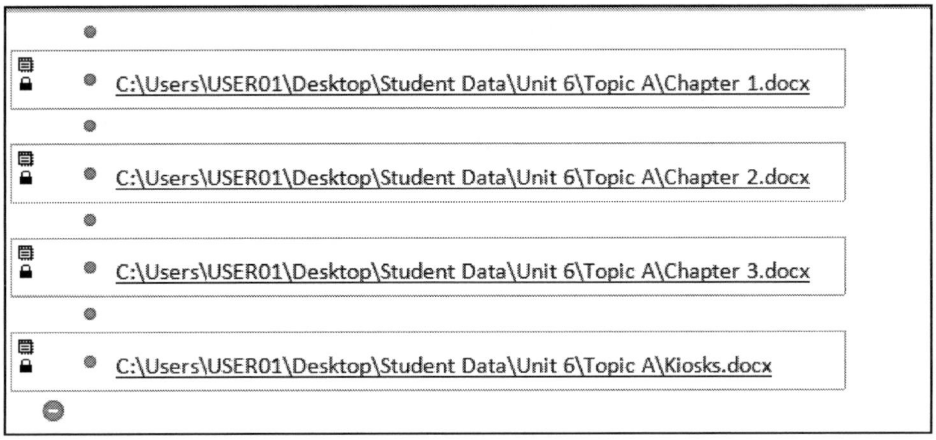

Exhibit 6-3: The collapsed subdocuments in Master Document view

Do it!

A-2: Working in Master Document view

Here's how	Here's why
1 Go to the top of the master document	
Observe the Subdocument icon	
	It's also shown in the upper-left corner of Exhibit 6-2 and Exhibit 6-4.
2 In the Master Document group, click **Collapse Subdocuments**	 The subdocuments now appear as hyperlinks, as shown in Exhibit 6-3. If you click a hyperlink, the subdocument will open in its own window.
3 Press CTRL and point to the hyperlink for the first subdocument	The pointer changes to a pointing hand, indicating that you can click the link.

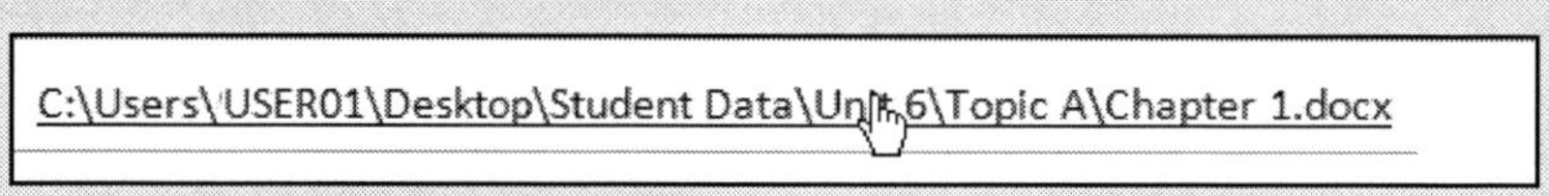

Here's how	Here's why
Click the link	To open the Chapter 1 document in its own window.
Release CTRL	
4 Click the **File** tab and click **Close**	To close the Chapter 1 document, returning to My master, which contains the subdocuments.
5 Click **Expand Subdocuments**	 (In the Master Document group.) To expand the subdocuments.

Deleting subdocuments

Explanation

You can delete a subdocument by selecting it and pressing Delete. To select a subdocument, click its Subdocument icon. It's located in the upper-left corner of the subdocument, as shown in Exhibit 6-4.

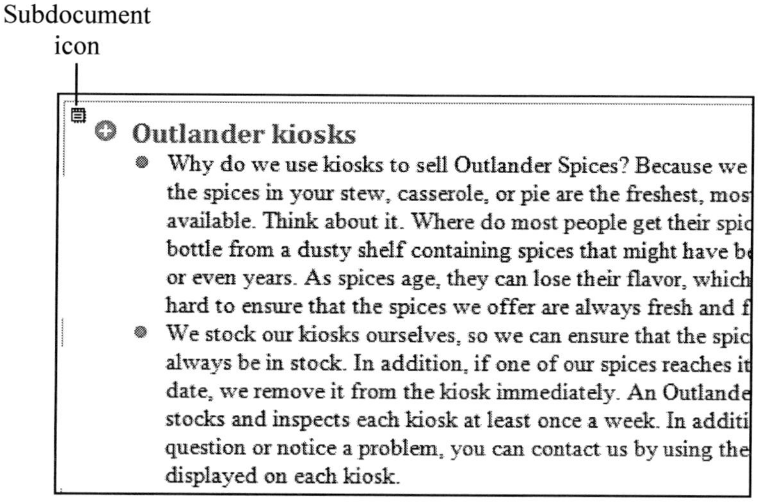

Exhibit 6-4: Part of a subdocument and its icon

Do it!

A-3: Deleting a subdocument

Here's how	Here's why
1 Scroll to the beginning of Kiosks	(This section begins with the heading "Outlander kiosks.") Because the information in this subdocument is not relevant, you'll delete it.
2 Click the subdocument icon, as shown	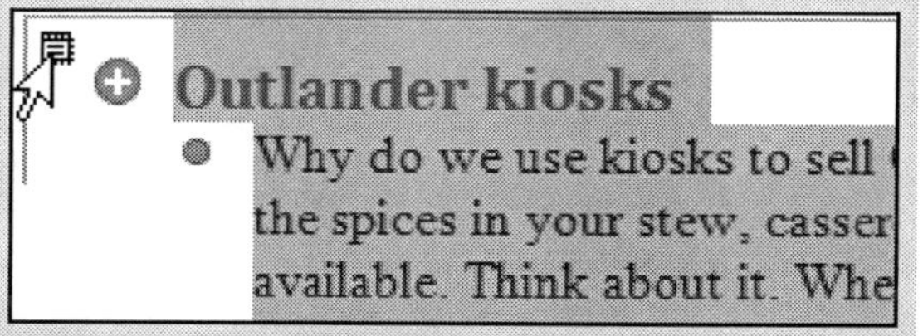 To select the subdocument.
3 Press DELETE	To delete the subdocument.
4 Update the document	

Adding a cover page to a document

Explanation

You can add a cover page to enhance the visual appeal of a document. To insert a cover page, click the Insert tab. In the Pages group, click Cover Page and select a design from the gallery. The gallery is shown in Exhibit 6-5.

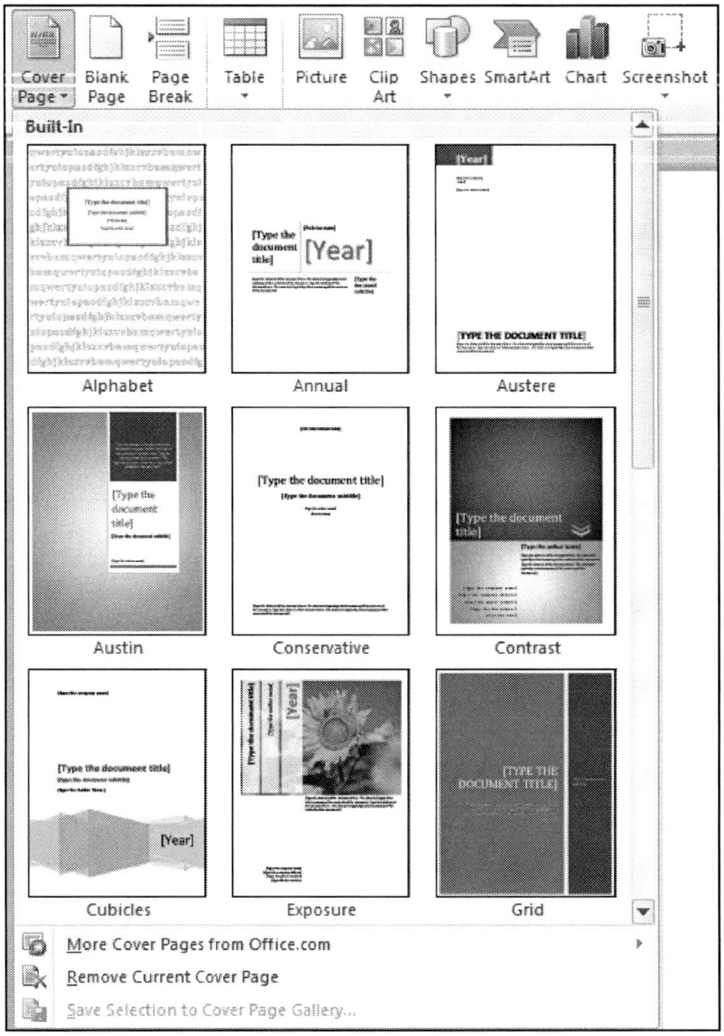

Exhibit 6-5: The gallery of cover pages

The page is automatically inserted at the beginning of your document, regardless of where the insertion point is when you insert the page. On the new cover page, click a placeholder, such as “Type the document subtitle,” and enter the text you want. An example is shown in Exhibit 6-6.

Exhibit 6-6: A cover page

Do it!

A-4: Adding a cover page

Here's how	Here's why
1 In the status bar, click the Print Layout button	 To switch to Print Layout view. The subdocuments are separated by section breaks.
2 Click the **Insert** tab	
3 In the Pages group, click **Cover Page**	To display a gallery of cover pages.
Select **Pinstripes**	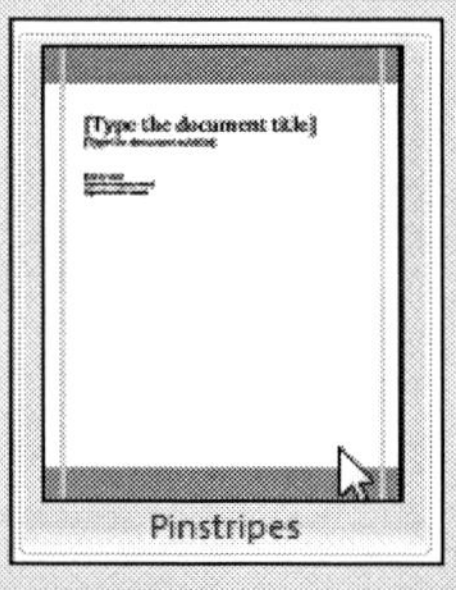 (Scroll in the gallery.) To insert a cover page at the beginning of the document.
4 Click **Type the document title**	To select the title placeholder.
Enter **Outlander Spices**	To create the title.
5 Click **Type the document subtitle**	To select the subtitle placeholder.
Enter **All About Spices**	To create the subtitle.
6 Click **Pick the date**	
Click the drop-down arrow	(To the right of "Pick the date.") To open a calendar.
Click today's date	To enter the date on the cover page.
7 Click **Type the company name**	
Enter **Outlander Spices**	
8 Update and close the document	

Topic B: Tables of contents and figures

This topic covers the following Microsoft Office Specialist objectives for exam 77-881: Word 2010.

#	Objective
4.1	**Insert and format pictures in a document**
	4.1.1 Add captions
4.2	**Insert and format shapes, WordArt, and SmartArt**
	4.2.3 Add captions
4.3	**Insert and format Clip Art**
	4.3.2 Add captions
6.3	**Create a Table of Contents in a document**
	6.3.1 Use default formats
	6.3.2 Set levels
	6.3.3 Set alignment
	6.3.4 Set tab leaders
	6.3.5 Modify styles
	6.3.6 Update a table of contents
	6.3.6.1 Page numbers
	6.3.6.2 Entire table

Generating a table of contents

Explanation

You can use Word to generate a table of contents from headings in a document, as shown in Exhibit 6-7. To be included in the table of contents, the text must be formatted with a heading style, such as Heading 1 or Heading 2. (Make sure that the heading styles are applied before you create the table of contents.)

To navigate directly to the associated content, press Ctrl and click an entry in the table of contents.

You can select a table-of-contents format from a gallery of style options. To display the gallery, shown in Exhibit 6-8, click the References tab and click Table of Contents. Then select the desired style. You can also specify such settings as alignment, tab leader, and style. To do so:

1. Click the References tab.
2. Click Table of Contents and choose Insert Table of Contents to open the Table of Contents dialog box.
3. By default, page numbers are shown, and they are right-aligned with a dotted tab leader. If desired, clear "Show page numbers" or "Right align page numbers." You can also select a different option from the Tab leader list.
4. Click Options if you want to specify the style used for each level in the table of contents.
5. Click Modify if you want to specify the style used for the table of contents.

Table of Contents

Exhibit 6-7: A table of contents generated from document headings

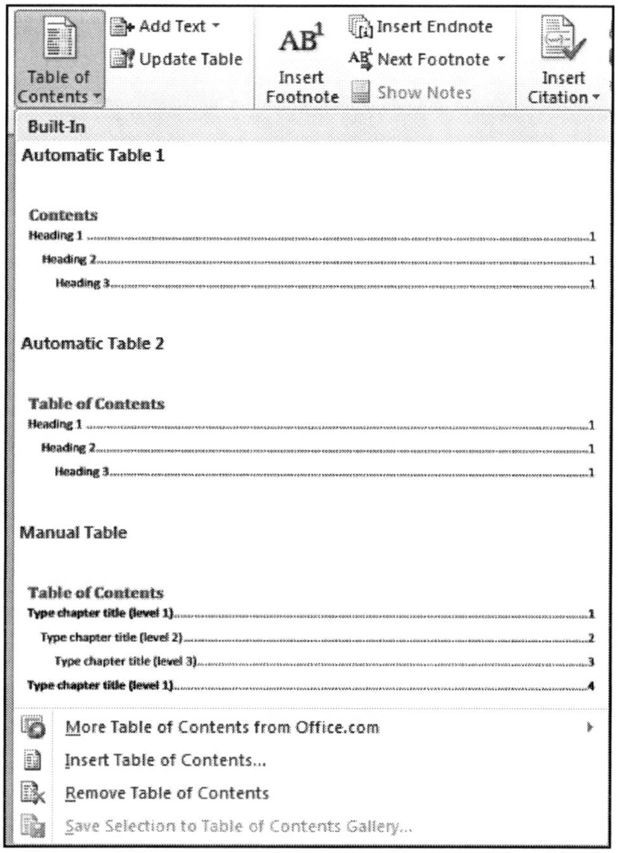

Exhibit 6-8: The Table of Contents gallery

Updating a table of contents

Word does not automatically update a table of contents as you change the contents of the document. So if you edit headings or move content, for example, you'll need to update the table of contents. You can open the Update Table of Contents dialog box, shown in Exhibit 6-9, by using either of these methods:

- On the References tab, in the Table of Content group, click Update Table.
- Select the table of contents. In the upper-left corner of the frame, click Update Table.

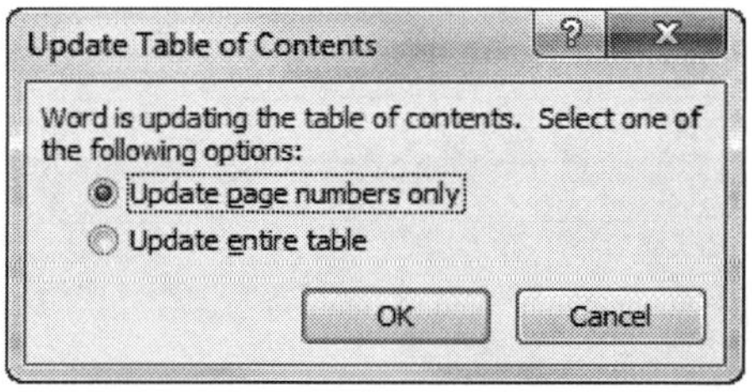

Exhibit 6-9: The Update Table of Contents dialog box

You can also change the format of a table of contents:

1. Select the table of contents.
2. In the upper-left corner of the table-of-contents frame, click the Table of Contents button.
3. In the gallery of styles, select the desired format.

Do it!

B-1: Creating and modifying a table of contents

The files for this activity are in Student Data folder **Unit 6\Topic B**.

Here's how	Here's why
1 Open Tables	
Save the document as **My tables**	
Place the insertion point at the top of page 2	This is a blank page. You'll insert a table of contents here.
2 Click the **References** tab	
3 In the Table of Contents group, click **Table of Contents**	To display the gallery of style options.
Select **Automatic Table 2**	To add a table of contents to the document.
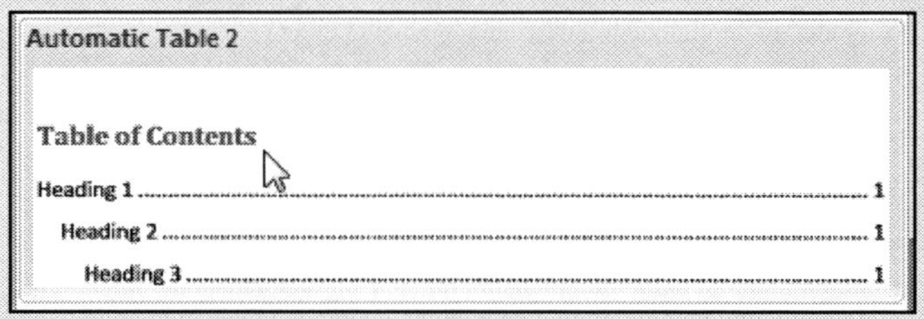	
4 Observe the table of contents	The section titled "Bay leaf" is on page 5.
5 Press and hold CTRL, and click **Bay leaf**	The insertion point moves to the "Bay leaf" content.
Release CTRL	
6 Edit the heading to read **Bay leaves**	On page 5.
Scroll to view the table of contents	(On page 2.) It has not been updated.
7 In the Table of Contents group, click **Update Table**	 To open the Update Table of Contents dialog box, shown in Exhibit 6-9. You can update page numbers only or the entire table.
Select **Update entire table**	To specify that both the text and the page numbers should be updated.
Click **OK**	To update the table of contents to reflect the heading change.

8	Click the table of contents	To select it.
9	Click the Table of Contents button, as shown	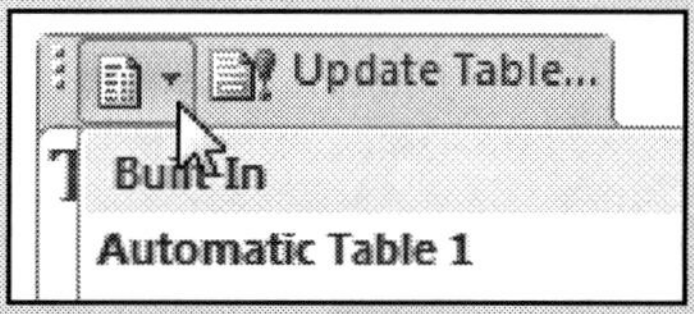 To display the gallery. You want to select a different format for the table of contents.
10	Select **Automatic Table 1**	To change the format of the table.
	Update the document	

Adding entries to a table of contents

Explanation

Suppose that your document changes after you have created its table of contents. For example, you add a new heading or chapter. You might want to include this new information in the table of contents.

To add text to an existing table of contents:

1. In the document, select the text you want to add.
2. On the References tab, in the Table of Contents group, click Add Text.
3. Select the appropriate heading level.
4. In the document, click in the table of contents to select it.
5. Click Update Table, select “Update entire table,” and click OK.

Do it!

B-2: Adding text to a table of contents

Here’s how	Here’s why
1 Place the insertion point at the top of page 3	To the left of the heading “Introduction.”
Enter **The history of spices**	To add a heading. You’d now like to include this heading in the table of contents.
Press ENTER	To place “Introduction” on another line.
2 Click within **The history of spices**	To place the insertion point in the heading.
In the Table of Contents group, click **Add Text**	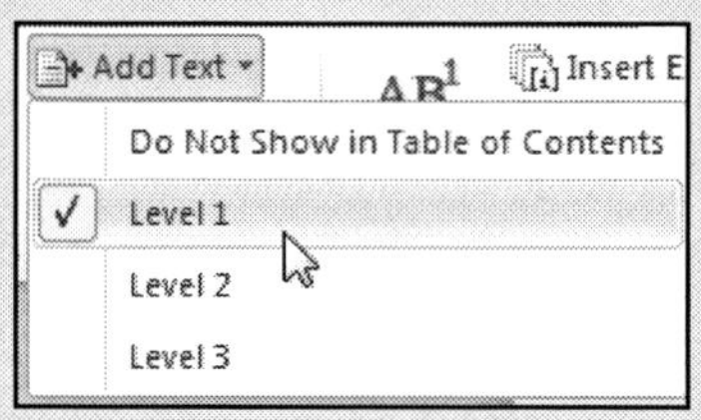
Choose **Level 1**	To specify the heading level.
3 Move to page 2	Notice that the heading is not automatically included in the table of contents.
Click anywhere in the table of contents	To select it.
4 Click **Update Table**	
Select **Update entire table**	
Click **OK**	To include the new heading in the table of contents.

Using captions to identify graphic elements

Explanation

You can add captions to tables and figures to identify them. All captions in Word begin with a *label*, which is the text that appears before a caption name. Word provides default labels, such as "Figure" and "Table." You can also create custom labels.

To add captions to figures or tables:

1. Select the figure or table for which you want to add a caption.
2. On the References tab, in the Captions group, click Insert Caption to open the Caption dialog box.
3. Click the New Label button if you want to change the label. Figure is the default label, as shown in Exhibit 6-10.
4. In the Caption box, enter the desired caption text.
5. Click OK.

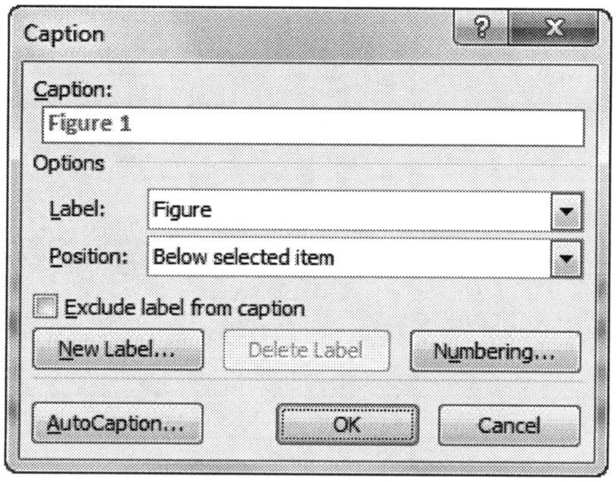

Exhibit 6-10: The Caption dialog box

Do it!

B-3: Adding captions

Here's how	Here's why
1 Select the bay leaves image, as shown	 Located on page 5.
2 In the Captions group, click **Insert Caption**	 (On the References tab.) To open the Caption dialog box. By default, "Figure 1" is the caption, and "Figure" is the label. Word automatically numbers the captions in sequential order. Also, the caption is placed below the image.
3 Edit the Caption box to read **Figure 1: Dried bay leaves**	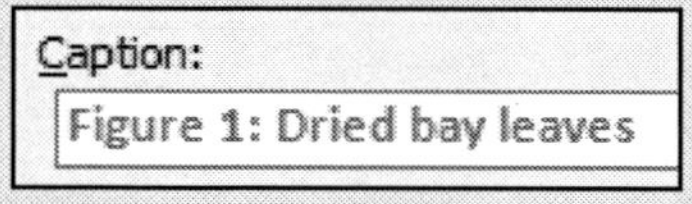
Click **OK**	The caption appears below the selected image.
4 Select the cinnamon image	On page 6.
5 Open the Caption dialog box	(Click Insert Caption.) The caption label is automatically numbered 2.
Edit the Caption box to read **Figure 2: Cinnamon sticks**	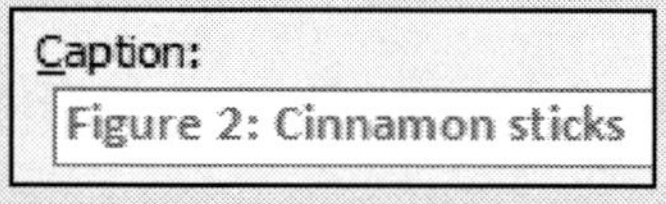
Click **OK**	To add the caption "Figure 2: Cinnamon sticks" below the selected image.
6 For the Cloves image, add the caption **Figure 3: Whole cloves**	
7 Update the document	

Generating a table of figures

Explanation

A *table of figures* is a list of elements, such as captioned pictures, that appear in a document. This table lists each element's caption and page number.

To add a table of figures:

1. In the Captions group on the References tab, click Insert Table of Figures to open the Table of Figures dialog box, shown in Exhibit 6-11.
2. Select the desired options.
3. Click OK.

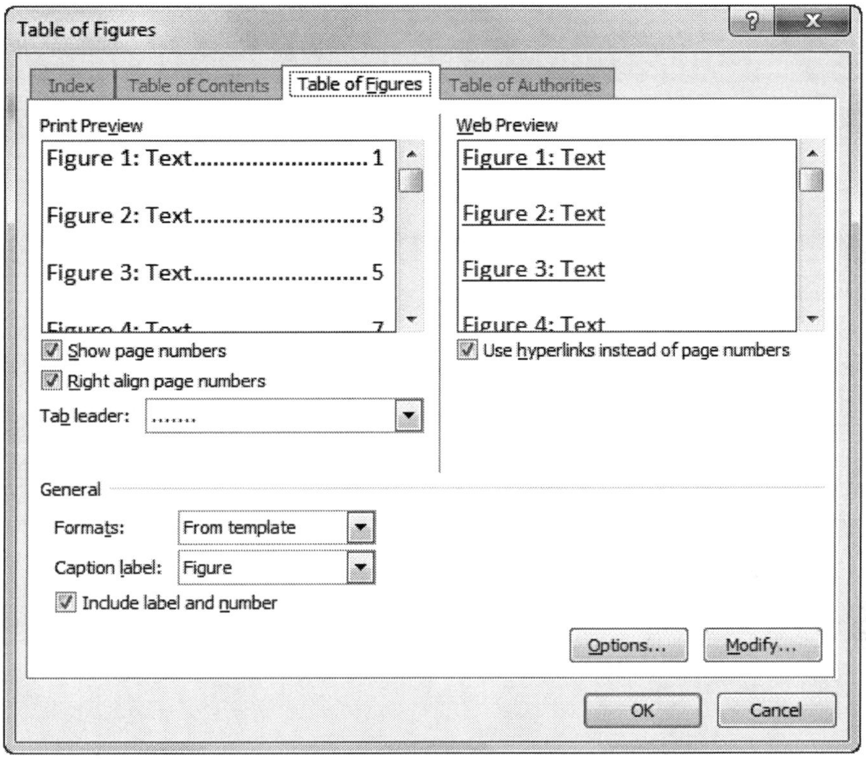

Exhibit 6-11: The Table of Figures dialog box

You can press Ctrl and click an item in the table to navigate directly to the associated figure.

Updating a table of figures

If your document changes, you might need to update its table of figures. Here's one way to do so:

1. Right-click the table of figures and choose Update Table.
2. Select "Update entire table" and click OK.

Do it!

B-4: Inserting and updating a table of figures

Here's how	Here's why
1 Move the insertion point to the end of the document	(Press Ctrl+End.) You'll insert a table of figures here.
2 In the Captions group, click **Insert Table of Figures**	(On the References tab.) To open the Table of Figures dialog box.
Click **OK**	To insert the table of figures.
3 Press CTRL and click **Whole cloves**	To go to the image of cloves.
4 Move to page 8	This page contains the image of coriander.
For the Coriander image, add the caption **Figure 4: Coriander**	
5 Move to the end of the document	To view the table of figures. Notice that the new caption has not been added.
6 Click the table of figures	To select it.
In the Captions group, click **Update Table**	To open the Update Table of Figures dialog box.
7 Select **Update entire table**	
Click **OK**	To add the new caption to the table.
8 Update and close the document	

Topic C: Indexes, bibliographies, and other references

This topic covers the following Microsoft Office Specialist objectives for exam 77-881: Word 2010.

#	Objective
3.1	**Apply and manipulate Page Setup settings**
	3.1.8 Insert a blank page into a document
6.2	**Create endnotes and footnotes in a document**
	6.2.1 Demonstrate the difference between endnotes and footnotes
	6.2.2 Manage footnote and endnote locations
	6.2.3 Configure footnote and endnote formats
	6.2.4 Presentation
	6.2.5 Change footnote and endnote numbering

This topic covers the following Microsoft Office Specialist objectives for exam 77-887: Word Expert 2010.

#	Objective
3.2	**Create a reference page**
	3.2.1 Add citations
	3.2.2 Manage sources
	3.2.3 Compile a bibliography
3.3	**Create a Table of Authorities in a document**
	3.3.1 Apply default formats
	3.3.2 Adjust alignment
	3.3.3 Apply a tab leader
	3.3.4 Modify styles
	3.3.5 Mark citations
	3.3.6 Use passim (short form)
3.4	**Create an index in a document**
	3.4.1 Specify the index type
	3.4.2 Specify columns
	3.4.3 Specify the language
	3.4.4 Modify an index
	3.4.5 Mark index entries

Indexing a document

Explanation

You can use Word to mark index entries and to generate an index from those entries. You can create an index entry for a word, a phrase, a symbol, or even for a topic that spans a range of pages.

To create an index, you first need to mark the index entries in a document. There are two types of index entries: main entries and subentries. A *main index entry* refers to a key concept or term. A *subentry* refers to a concept or term that's related to the main entry. Main entries are required; subentries are optional.

Marking index entries

To mark an index entry:

1 Select the text that you want to include in the index.

2 On the References tab, in the Index group, click Mark Entry to open the Mark Index Entry dialog box, shown in Exhibit 6-12. The Main entry box contains the text you selected.

3 Enter text in the Subentry box to create a subentry, if necessary.

4 Click Mark to mark the selected text and to insert an XE field in the document.

   XE is an Index Entry field, which specifies the text and page number for an index entry. The field code is enclosed in curly braces, { }, and the field is formatted as hidden text.

5 Click Close to close the Mark Index Entry dialog box.

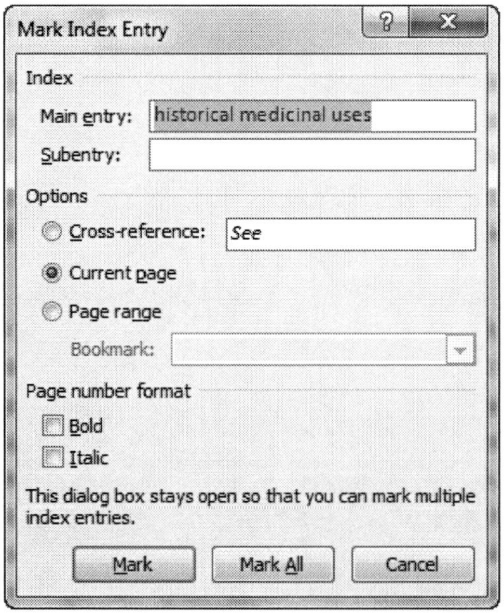

Exhibit 6-12: The Mark Index Entry dialog box

Do it!

C-1: Creating main index entries and subentries

The files for this activity are in Student Data folder **Unit 6\Topic C**.

Here's how	Here's why
1 Open Index	
Save the document as **My index**	
2 View the body text under "The historical medicinal use of spices"	This heading is on page 1.
In the heading, select **historical medicinal uses**	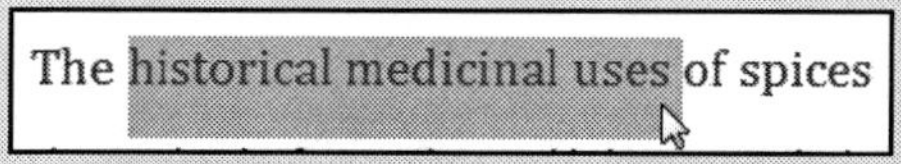 You'll mark this text as a main index entry.
3 In the Index group, click **Mark Entry**	 (On the References tab.) To open the Mark Index Entry dialog box, shown in Exhibit 6-12.
Click **Mark**	

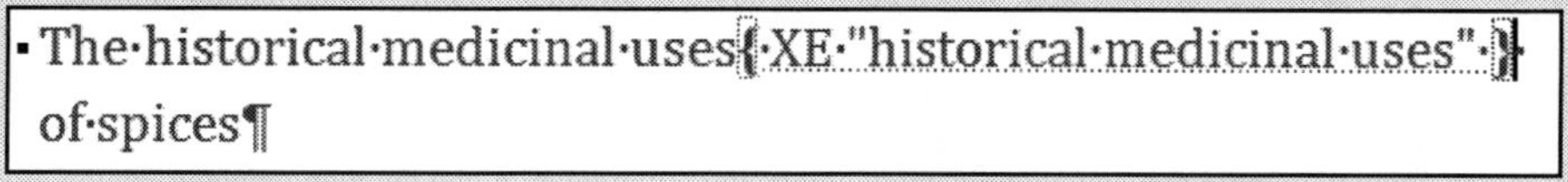

Here's how	Here's why
	The XE field, which defines the text and page number for an index entry, is added to the document. The field is formatted as hidden text, and the field code is enclosed in braces. The Mark Index Entry dialog box remains open so you can add more entries. You'll add a subentry.
4 In the second paragraph below the heading, select **healing wounds**	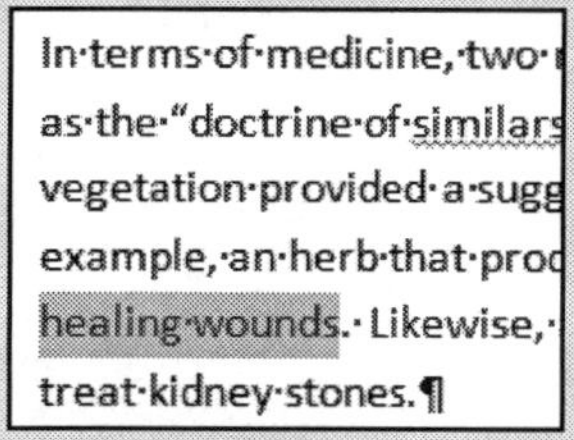 (At the end of the third sentence. You might need to move the dialog box.) You'll copy this text so you can paste it into the Subentry box.
Press CTRL + C	To copy the selection.
Click the Subentry box and press CTRL + V	To paste the new entry as a subentry in the Mark Index Entry dialog box. The selected text also appears in the Main entry box.

5 Edit the Main entry box to read **historical medicinal uses**

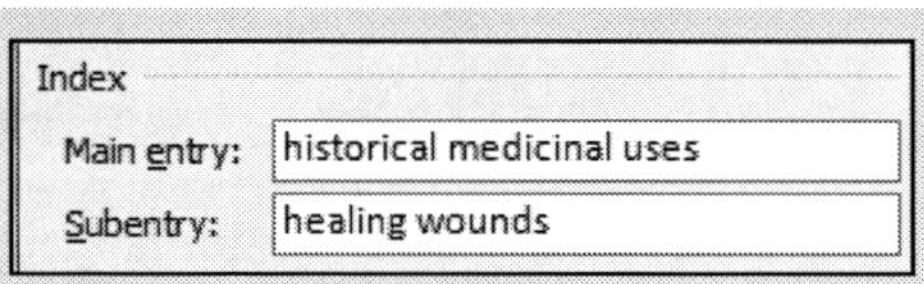

Click **Mark**

6 In the next paragraph, mark **fever** as a subentry, with **historical medicinal uses** as the main entry

(In the second sentence.) Select "fever," copy it, and paste it into the Subentry box. Edit the Main entry box and click Mark.

7 On the next page, mark **modern medicine** as a main index entry

In the heading, select "modern medicine," activate the Mark Index Entry dialog box, and click Mark.

Next you'll add several subentries.

8 In the second paragraph below the heading, select **antioxidants**

Edit the Subentry box to read **antioxidants**

Copy the text and paste it into the Subentry box.

Edit the Main entry box to read **modern medicine**

Click **Mark**

To complete the entry. Next, you'll add two more subentries that are in the same paragraph.

9 Mark **cancer** and **heart disease** as subentries, with **modern medicine** as the main entry

(These terms are in the sentence with "antioxidants.") Select "cancer," copy it and paste it into the Subentry box, edit the Main entry box, and click Mark. Follow the same steps for "heart disease."

Many·spices·contain·direct·health·benefits.·Cloves,·cinnamon,·and·oregano·have·been· found·to·contain·high·levels·of·antioxidants{·XE·"modern·medicine:antioxidants"·},· which·may·help·prevent·damage·to·cells·in·the·body·that·could·lead·to·cancer{·XE· "modern·medicine:cancer"·},·heart·disease{·XE·"modern·medicine:heart·disease"·},· Alzheimer's·disease,·and·Parkinson's·disease.·Granted,·you·aren't·likely·to·consume· enough·cinnamon·to·provide·a·tangible·prevention·against·cancer,·but·it's·reassuring·to· know·that·our·spices·contain·some·of·the·same·healthy·ingredients·as·beans,· blueberries,·and·apples.¶

Click **Close**

To close the Mark Index Entry dialog box.

10 Update the document

Creating indexes

Explanation

After you've marked index entries in a document, you can generate an index. To do so:

1. Place the insertion point where you want the index to appear.
2. On the References tab, in the Index group, click the Insert Index button to open the Index dialog box, shown in Exhibit 6-13.
3. Select an index style from the Formats list.
4. Specify any additional settings as needed.
   - Select an index type. *Indented* displays subentries indented below a main entry. *Run-in* displays subentries on the same line as the main entry, separated with a colon or semicolon.
   - Select the number of columns you want the index to use.
   - From the Language list, specify the desired language for the index.
   - Check "Right align page numbers," if desired. If this option is checked, you can select a leader character from the Tab leader list.
   - Click Modify if you want to specify or modify the style used for the index.
5. Click OK.

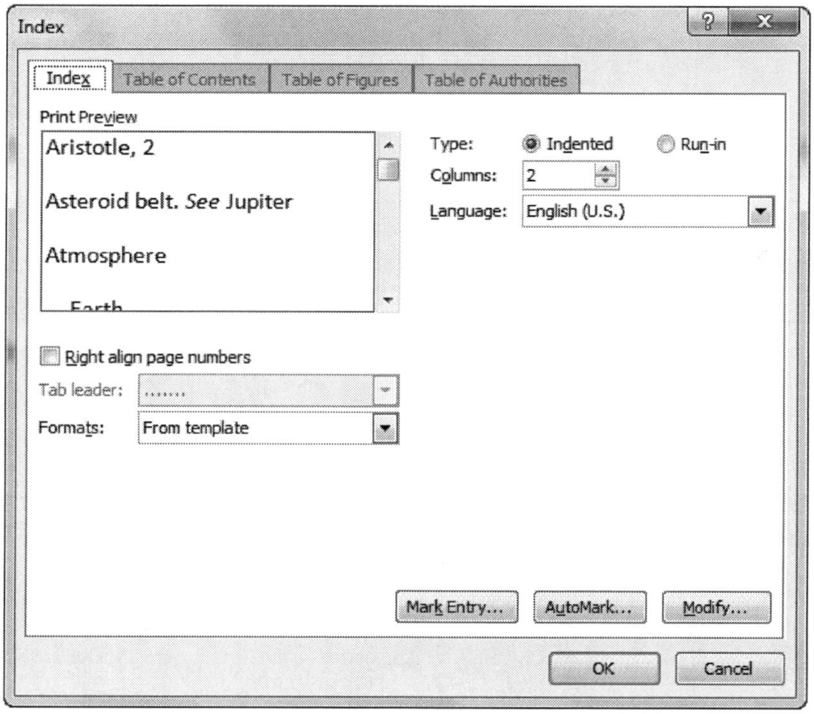

Exhibit 6-13: The Index dialog box

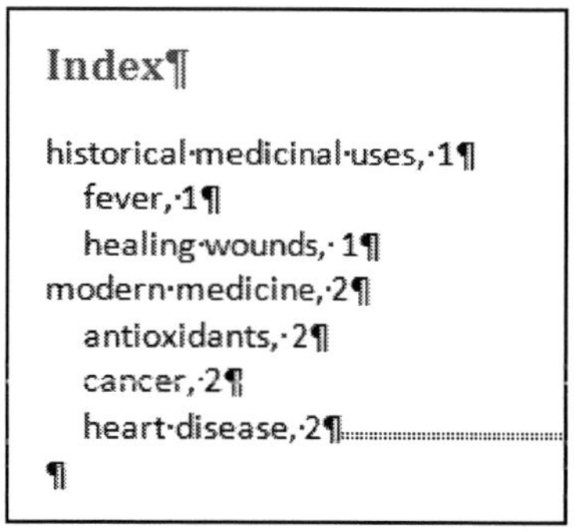
Index¶
historical·medicinal·uses,·1¶
fever,·1¶
healing·wounds,·1¶
modern·medicine,·2¶
antioxidants,·2¶
cancer,·2¶
heart·disease,·2¶
¶

Exhibit 6-14: A generated index

Do it!

C-2: Generating an index

Here's how	Here's why
1 Place the insertion point at the end of the document	
2 In the Index group, click **Insert Index**	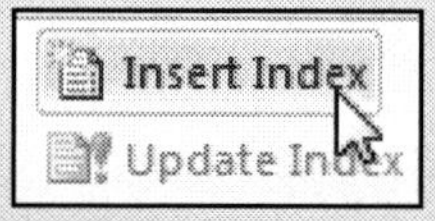 (On the References tab.) To open the Index dialog box.
3 Next to Type, verify that **Indented** is selected	To specify how subentries will appear in the index.
In the Columns box, enter **1**	To specify that the index items appear in a single column on the page.
Click **OK**	To create the index, as shown in Exhibit 6-14.
4 Update and close the document	

Citations

Explanation

A *citation* is a reference to a book, journal article, or other source of information included in a document. Citations include such information as the type of source (book, journal article, report, etc.), the author's name, the title, the year published, and the publisher. When your document is completed, Word can compile all citation information and present it in a bibliography.

First, select the style you want to use for your citations. You can select from such styles as MLA, APA, or the *Chicago Manual of Style*. For example, if you're creating a social sciences document, you'll generally want to select either the MLA or APA style. To specify a style, click the References tab. Then, in the Citations & Bibliography group, click the Style arrow and select the desired style from the list.

After you've selected a style, you can begin entering your sources. To add a citation:

1 Place the insertion point where you want the citation to appear.
2 Click the References tab.
3 In the Citation & Bibliography group, click Insert Citation and choose Add New Source to open the Create Source dialog box, shown in Exhibit 6-15. (If you want to add the detailed source information later, choose Add New Placeholder instead of Add New Source.)
4 Enter the source information in the dialog box. Check Show All Bibliography Fields to display additional fields, such as Editor, Edition, and Comments.
5 Click OK.

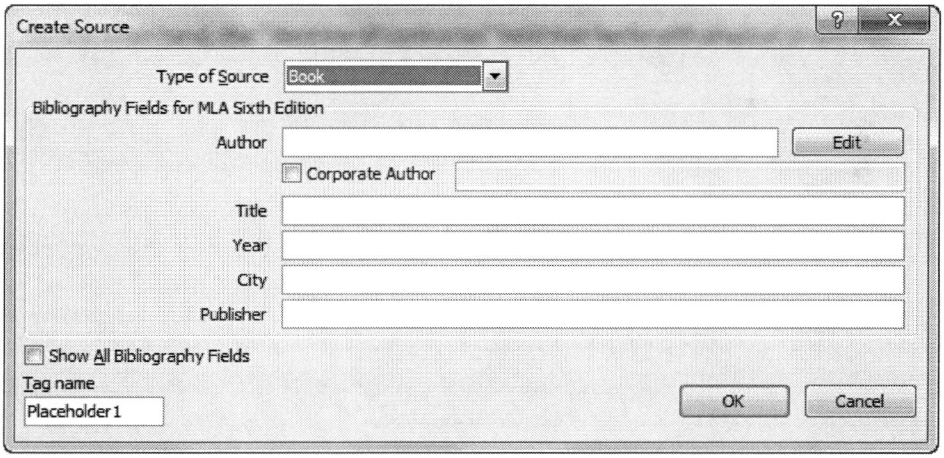

Exhibit 6-15: The Create Source dialog box

Do it!

C-3: Inserting a citation

The files for this activity are in Student Data folder **Unit 6\Topic C**.

	Here's how	Here's why
1	Open References	
	Save the document as **My references**	
2	Move the insertion point to the end of the section titled "The historical medicinal uses of spices," as shown	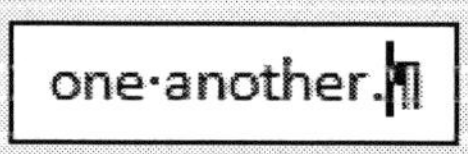 At the top of page 2.
	Press SPACEBAR	You'll add a citation here.
3	Click the **References** tab	
	In the Citations & Bibliography group, from the Style list, select **MLA Sixth Edition**	 To specify a citation style.
4	In the Citations & Bibliography group, click **Insert Citation**	
	Choose **Add New Source...**	To open the Create Source dialog box.
	In the Type of Source list, verify that **Book** is selected	
5	In the Author box, enter **Herbert Reese**	To record the name of the author of the work being cited.
6	In the Title box, enter **Ancient Medicine**	To specify the name of the work being cited.
	In the Year box, enter **1999**	To specify the year the work was published.
	In the City box, enter **New York**	To specify the publisher's location.
	In the Publisher box, enter **Culinary Press**	
7	Click **OK**	 To create the citation. The author's last name is shown in parentheses.

Generating a bibliography

Explanation

After you've inserted citations and sources, you can create a bibliography. A *bibliography* is a list of the sources cited in a document. Generally, this list appears at the end of a document.

To generate a bibliography:

1. Place the insertion point where you want the bibliography to appear, generally at the end of the document.
2. Click the References tab.
3. In the Citations & Bibliography group, click Bibliography.
4. From the gallery (shown in Exhibit 6-16), select a bibliography format, or choose Insert Bibliography if you want to further customize the format.

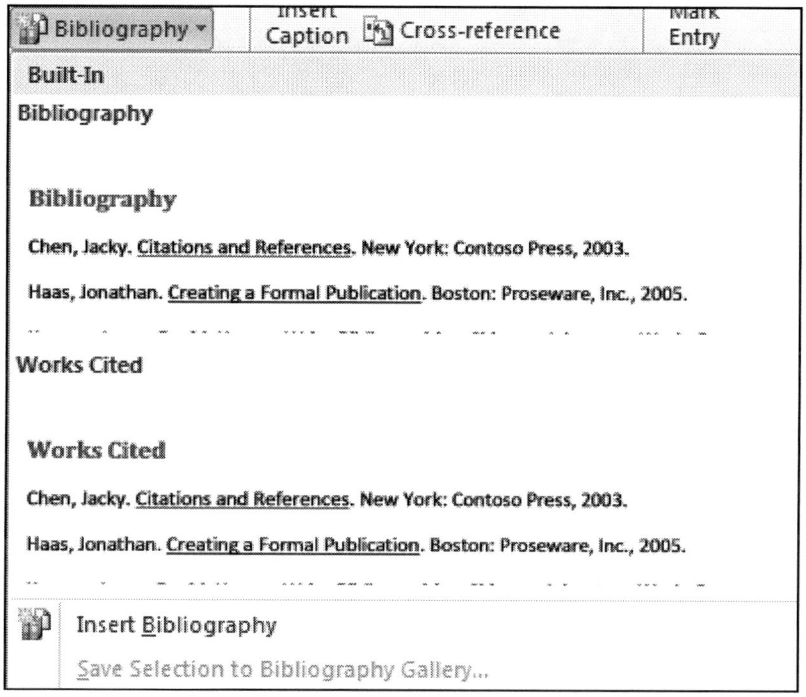

Exhibit 6-16: The Bibliography gallery

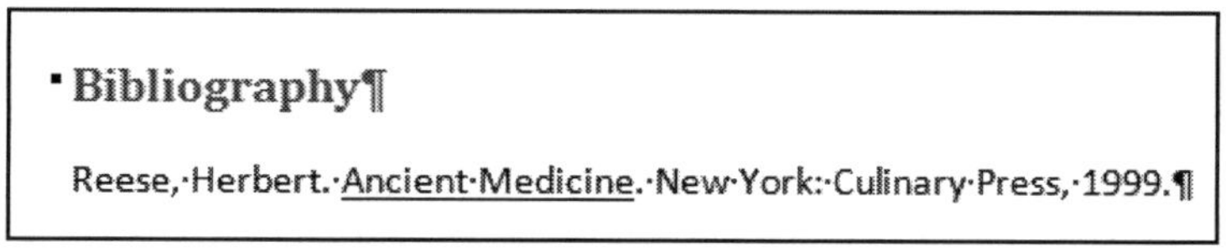

Exhibit 6-17: A bibliography entry using the MLA Sixth Edition format

Modifying sources and bibliographies

You can update or change source information. To do so, use the Edit Source dialog box.

1 On the References tab, in the Citations & Bibliography group, click Manage Sources to open the Source Manager dialog box, shown in Exhibit 6-18.
2 Under Master List, select the citation you want to change. Click Edit to open the Edit Source dialog box, shown in Exhibit 6-19.
3 Make the necessary changes and click OK.
4 If the source appears in both the master list and the current list (meaning that the source is in the current document), a message box asks if you want to update both lists. Click Yes.
5 Click Close to close the Source Manager dialog box.
6 Click the bibliography to select it, and then click Update Citations and Bibliography.

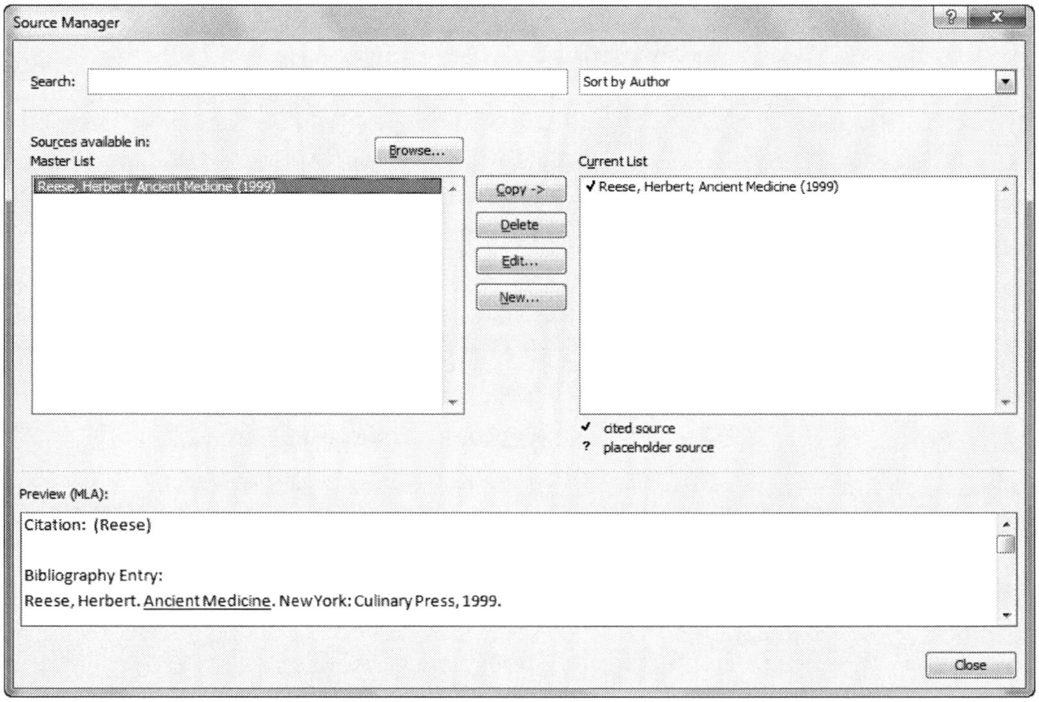

Exhibit 6-18: The Source Manager dialog box

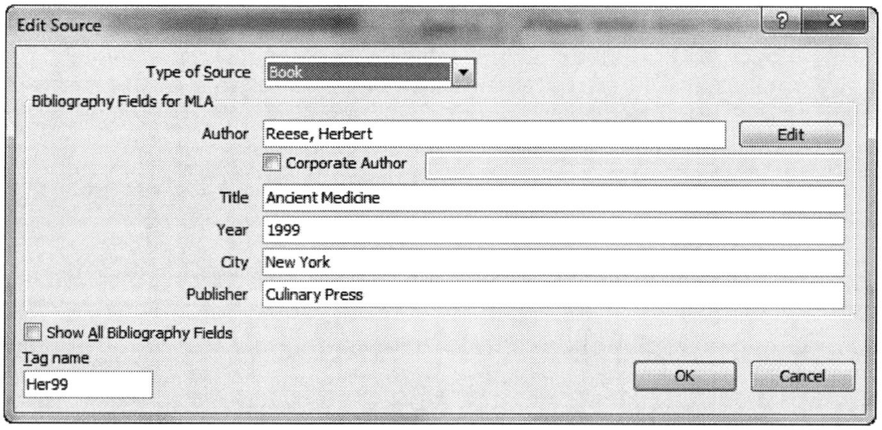

Exhibit 6-19: The Edit Source dialog box

The bibliographical sources each user creates are stored in the XML file "Sources" in the folder *%systemroot%*\Users*user_name*\AppData\Roaming\Microsoft\Bibliography. AppData is a hidden folder.

Do it!

C-4: Adding and modifying a bibliography

Here's how	Here's why
1 Move to the end of the document	
2 In the Citation & Bibliography group, click **Bibliography**	(On the References tab.) To display the gallery.
Select **Bibliography**	To add a list of sources cited in the document.
3 In the Citations & Bibliography group, click **Manage Sources**	To open the Source Manager dialog box.
Under Master List, select **Reese, Herbert; Ancient Medicine (1999)**	To select the source you want to change.
Click **Edit**	(This button is in the center of the dialog box.) To open the Edit Source dialog box.
4 Edit the Year box to read **2007**	 To update the year published.
5 Check **Show All Bibliography Fields**	To display additional fields.
6 Scroll to view the Comments field	The last bibliography field in the list.
In the Comments box, enter **See page 72**	To include a helpful comment for the reader.
Click **OK**	A message appears, asking if you want to update the master list of bibliography entries as well as the current document.
7 Click **Yes**	To update the source information.
Click **Close**	To close the Source Manager dialog box.

8 Observe the bibliography — It's not automatically updated.

Click the bibliography — To select it. A frame appears around it.

Click **Update Citations and Bibliography** — In the upper-left corner of the frame around the bibliography.

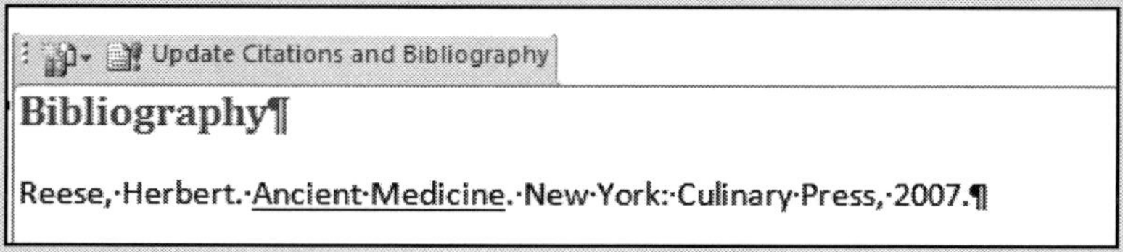

The bibliography is updated, so the citation displays the year 2007. However, the current style (MLA) doesn't display comments.

9 In the Citations & Bibliography group, from the Style list, select **ISO 690 – First Element and Date** — This style includes the comment.

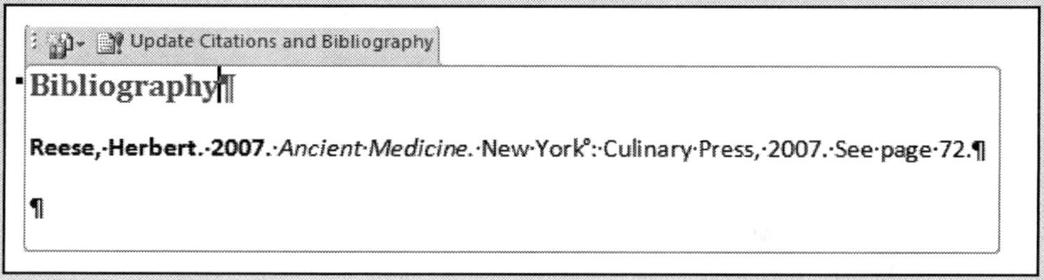

Update the document

Generating a table of authorities

Explanation

An *authority* is a specific kind of citation that refers to universally accepted expert sources, such as legal cases, statutes, treatises, regulations, or rules that are cited in a document. You can also create your own categories of authority.

A *table of authorities* is a list of information sources used in a document and their corresponding page numbers. To include an authority in a table, you must first mark it. To do so:

1. Select the text that you want to mark as a citation for the table of authorities.
2. On the References tab, in the Table of Authorities group, click Mark Citation to open the Mark Citation dialog box, shown in Exhibit 6-20.
3. To add a new category of authorities:
   a. Click Category to open the Edit Category dialog box.
   b. From the category list, select one of the available names to replace it. You can replace any name, but you might want to begin by replacing the generic categories that are named with numbers, from 8 through 16.
   c. In the Replace with box, enter the name of the category you want to add.
   d. Click Replace.
   e. Click OK to return to the Mark Citation dialog box.
4. From the Category list, select the category of your citation.
5. Modify any of the other fields, if necessary, to include more information. Then click Mark.
6. Click Close to close the Mark Citation dialog box.

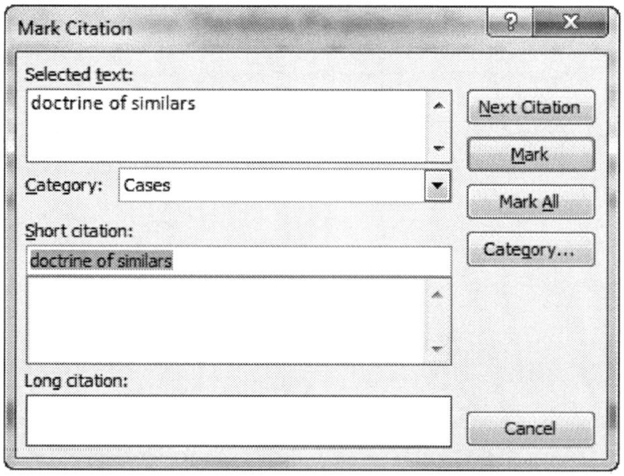

Exhibit 6-20: The Mark Citation dialog box

To create a table of authorities, place the insertion point where you want the table to appear, and on the References tab, click Insert Table of Authorities. The Table of Authorities dialog box, shown in Exhibit 6-21, opens. Select the desired options and click OK.

In the Table of Authorities dialog box, you can also specify a tab leader and formatting for the table. To do so:

- If passim is checked, Word will display "passim" rather than the page numbers for citations with five or more page references. Clear passim to display page numbers for all citations.
- From the Tab Leader list, select an option.
- From the Formats list, select an option to format the table.
- Click Modify if you want to specify or modify the style used for the table of authorities and the heading.

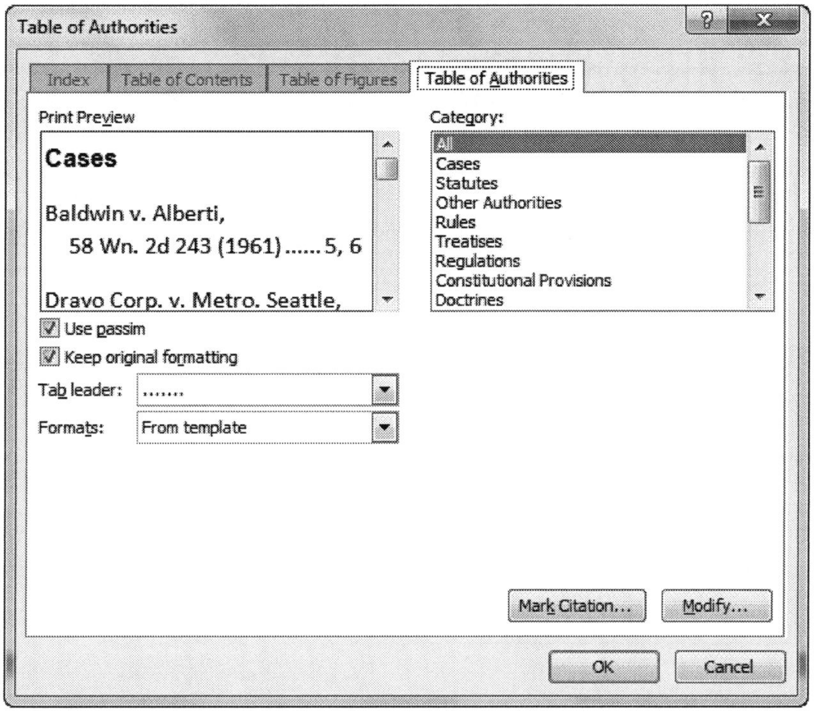

Exhibit 6-21: The Table of Authorities dialog box

To update the table, select it and click Update Table of Authorities in the Table of Authorities group on the References tab.

You can adjust the alignment and tab stops for a table of authorities after you've inserted it. To do so, select the table and apply the desired alignment setting in the Paragraph group on the Home tab, or adjust the tab stops on the ruler.

Do it!

C-5: Creating and updating a table of authorities

Here's how	Here's why
1 Move to the beginning of the document	Press Ctrl + Home.
In the second paragraph under the heading "The historical medicinal uses of spices," select **doctrine of similars**	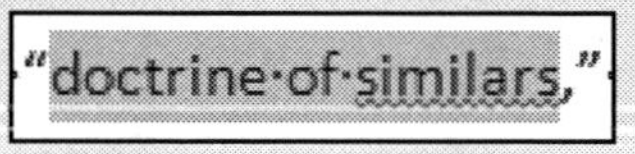 (Don't include the quotations in the selection.) This is the text you'll mark as an authority to be included in a table of authorities.
2 In the Table of Authorities group, click **Mark Citation**	 To open the Mark Citation dialog box. You want to create a category of authorities called "Doctrines."
3 Click **Category**	(This button is on the right side of the dialog box.) To open the Edit Category dialog box.
4 From the Category list, select **8**	(You might need to scroll.) You'll replace this category name.
In the Replace With box, enter **Doctrines**	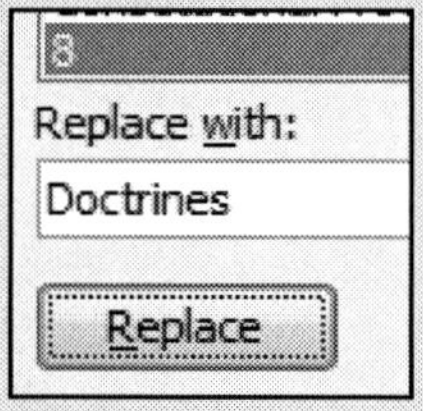 To specify the new name.
Click **Replace**	To replace "8" with "Doctrines."
Click **OK**	To return to the Mark Citation dialog box.
5 From the Category list, select **Doctrines**	To categorize this citation.
6 Click **Mark**	To mark the citation in the document.
Click **Close**	To close the Mark Citation dialog box. Notice the code added to the document to identify this citation. "TA" stands for "Table of Authorities." This code is not printed when you print the document.
7 Move to the end of the document	Press Ctrl+End.
Insert a new page	Press Ctrl+Enter.

8	In the Table of Authorities group, click **Insert Table of Authorities**	Insert Table of Authorities To open the Table of Authorities dialog box.
	Click **OK**	To create the table of authorities.
9	Move to the beginning of the document	
	In the third paragraph under the heading "The historical medicinal uses of spices," select **doctrine of contraries**	To select another term for the table of authorities.
10	Click **Mark Citation**	In the Table of Authorities group.
	In the Category list, verify that **Doctrines** is selected	
	Click **Mark**	To mark the citation.
	Click **Close**	
11	Move to the end of the document	
12	Click the table of authorities	To select it.
	In the Table of Authorities group, click Update Table	To update the table. The new entry appears in alphabetical order.

Doctrines¶

doctrine·of·contraries ....→............1¶
doctrine·of·similars ....→............1¶

Update the document

Footnotes and endnotes

Explanation

Footnotes and *endnotes* provide explanations about or references to information in a document. Footnotes appear at the bottom of a page, and endnotes appear at the end of a document. Word inserts a reference mark in the text where a footnote or endnote is inserted. This reference mark can be a number or a symbol.

To add a footnote:

1 Place the insertion point where you want the footnote reference mark to appear.
2 On the References tab, in the Footnotes group, click Insert Footnote to insert the footnote reference number. The insertion point moves to the bottom of the page so you can enter the footnote information.
3 Type the footnote information.

After adding footnotes, you can change the numbering style and other formats by using the Footnote and Endnote dialog box, shown in Exhibit 6-22. To open this dialog box, click the Dialog Box Launcher in the Footnotes group. You can specify number formats and the location of footnotes and endnotes. After specifying the settings you want, click Apply.

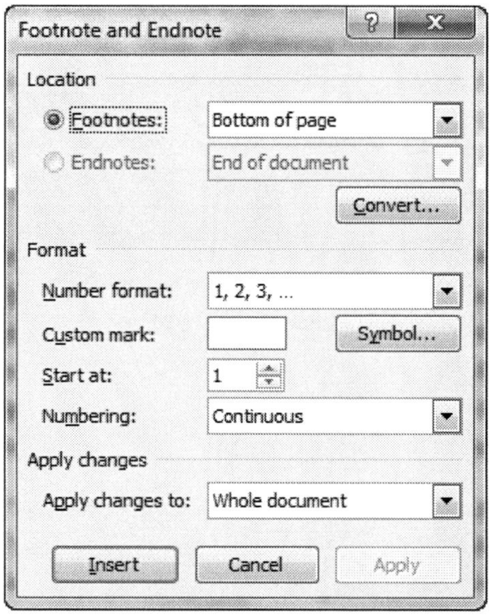

Exhibit 6-22: The Footnote and Endnote dialog box

Deleting footnotes

You can delete footnotes and endnotes when they are no longer needed. To do so, select a note's reference mark and press Delete. Both the reference mark and the note itself will be removed. When you delete footnotes and endnotes, you are not asked to confirm the deletion.

Do it!

C-6: Using footnotes

Here's how	Here's why
1 Move to the beginning of the document	You'll add a footnote on this page.
2 Place the insertion point at the end of the second paragraph below the heading "The historical medicinal uses of spices"	This sentence ends with "…might be used to treat kidney stones."
3 In the Footnotes group, click **Insert Footnote**	 (On the References tab.) To add a footnote. The number 1 appears where you placed the insertion point, and the footnote area appears at the bottom of the page.
4 Enter **This fundamental doctrine was first published in 1865.**	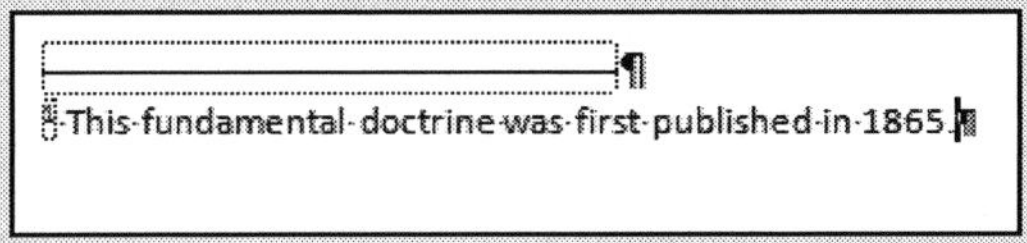
5 In the document, point to footnote number 1	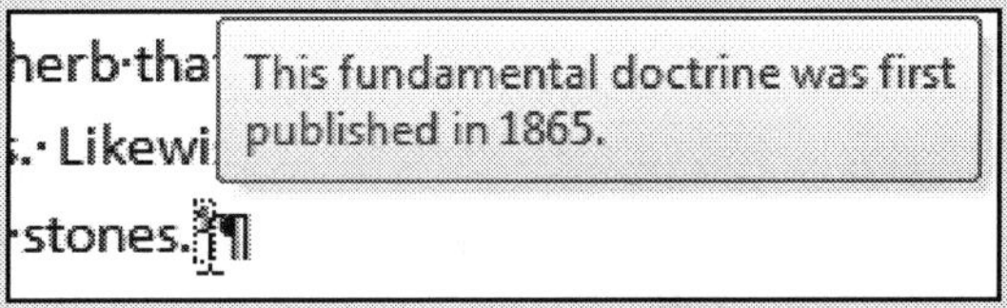 The footnote text appears as a comment.
6 View the document in Print Preview	The footnote appears at the bottom of the page.
Close Print Preview	You'll edit the footnote.
7 In the footnote, change the year to **1869**	
8 In the document, point to footnote number 1	The comment that appears reflects the updated text of the footnote. Next, you'll change the footnote number format to use uppercase letters.

9 In the Footnotes group, click the Dialog Box Launcher, as shown

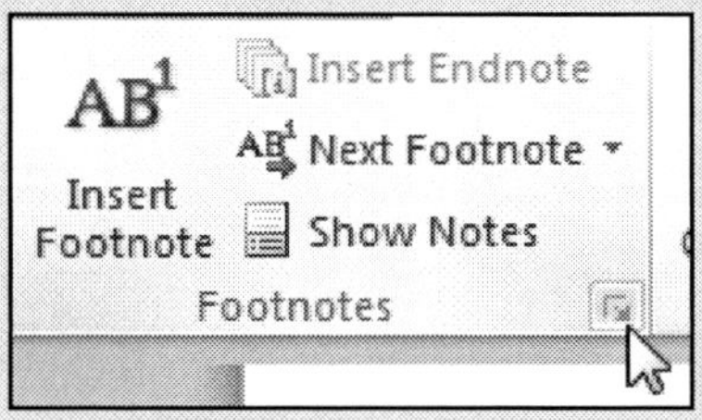

To open the Footnote and Endnote dialog box.

From the Number format list, select **A, B, C, …**

10 In the "Apply changes to" list, verify that **Whole document** is selected

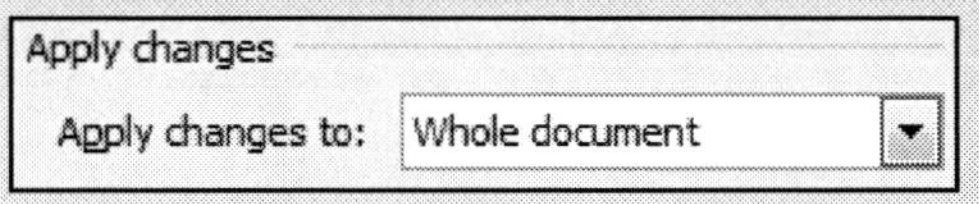

Click **Apply**

The footnote numbering reflects the change.

11 Select the footnote reference letter, as shown

On page 1.

Press DELETE

The footnote reference letter and its associated footnote both disappear.

12 Update and close the document

Topic D: Bookmarks and cross-references

This topic covers the following Microsoft Office Specialist objectives for exam 77-881: Word 2010.

#	Objective
6.1	**Create endnotes and footnotes in a document**
	6.1.2 Use a hyperlink as a bookmark

This topic covers the following Microsoft Office Specialist objectives for exam 77-887: Word Expert 2010.

#	Objective
3.2	**Create a reference page**
	3.2.4 Apply cross-references

Adding bookmarks

Explanation

You can use a *bookmark* to mark a location in a document, which you can then navigate to directly by clicking the associated bookmark entry in the Bookmark dialog box. You can add bookmarks to specific locations, text, or objects. You can create references to these bookmarks from any section of a document by using *cross-references*.

By using bookmarks, you can quickly find specific sections of a document without searching for them. Bookmarks are useful when you're working in a long document. To add a bookmark:

1. Place the insertion point where you want to add the bookmark.
2. On the Insert tab, in the Links group, click Bookmark to open the Bookmark dialog box, shown in Exhibit 6-23.
3. In the Bookmark name box, enter a name for the bookmark. Bookmark names must begin with a letter; numbers are allowed after the first character. Spaces are not allowed in bookmark names.
4. Click Add.

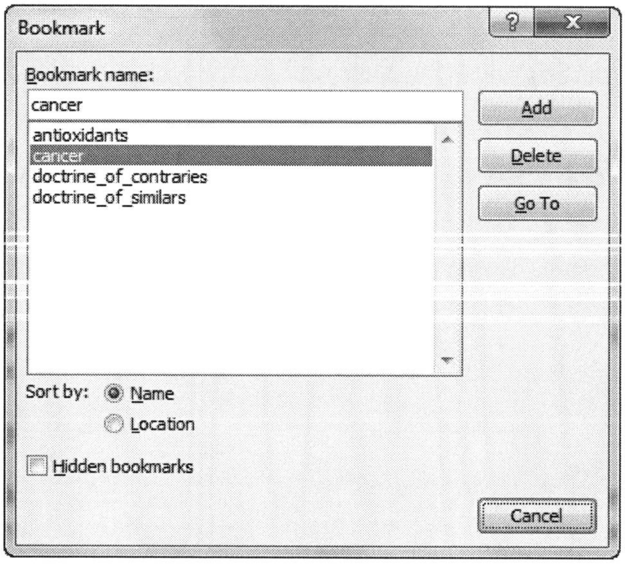

Exhibit 6-23: The Bookmark dialog box

Do it!

D-1: Creating bookmarks

The files for this activity are in Student Data folder **Unit 6\Topic D**.

Here's how	Here's why
1 Open Bookmarks	
Save the document as **My bookmarks**	
2 On the Home tab, click ¶	To hide the paragraph marks. You'll add bookmarks for several words.
3 Verify that the insertion point is on page 1	(This page contains the heading "The historical medicinal uses of spices.") You'll insert two bookmarks for text on this page.
Select **doctrine of similars**	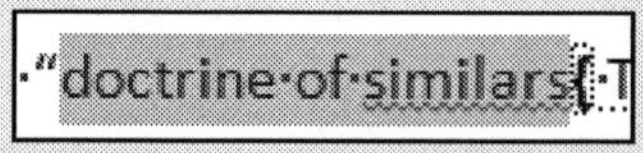 In the second paragraph below the heading "The historical medicinal uses of spices."
4 Click the **Insert** tab	

5 In the Links group, click **Bookmark**	 To open the Bookmark dialog box.
In the Bookmark name box, enter **doctrine_of_similars**	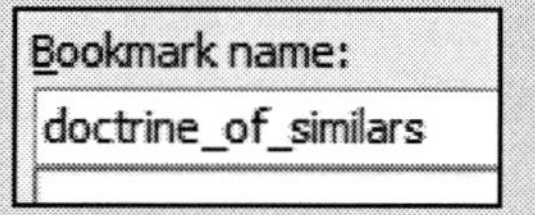
Click **Add**	To close the Bookmark dialog box and add the bookmark.
6 Select **doctrine of contraries**	 In the following paragraph.
Open the Bookmark dialog box	In the Links group, click Bookmark.
Edit the Bookmark name box to read **doctrine_of_contraries**	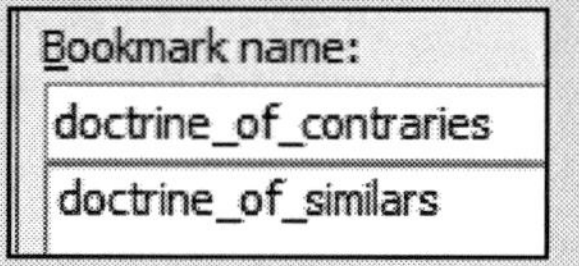 To specify a name for the next bookmark.
Add the bookmark	Click Add.
7 On the next page, add bookmarks for **antioxidants** and **cancer**	(Both words are in the second paragraph after the heading "Spices as modern medicine.") Select the text, open the Bookmark dialog box, enter the name, and click Add.
8 Update the document	

Using bookmarks

Explanation

After you've added bookmarks to a document, you can use the Bookmark dialog box to navigate directly to any bookmark. Here's how:

1. In the Links group, click Bookmark to open the Bookmark dialog box.
2. Under Bookmark name, select the desired bookmark.
3. Click Go To.

Do it!

D-2: Navigating to bookmarks in a document

Here's how	Here's why
1 Place the insertion point at the end of the document	
2 In the Links group, click **Bookmark**	To open the Bookmark dialog box.
In the list under Bookmark name, select **antioxidants**	To select the bookmark you want to navigate to.
Click **Go To**	To move the insertion point to "antioxidants," where you added the bookmark.
3 Experiment with navigating to other bookmarks	
4 Click **Close**	To close the Bookmark dialog box.
5 Update the document	

Deleting bookmarks

Explanation

When you want to delete a bookmark, you select it in the Bookmark dialog box and click Delete. You will not be prompted to confirm the deletion. If you mistakenly delete a bookmark, you will have to add it again. After deleting a bookmark, click Close to close the Bookmark dialog box.

Do it!

D-3: Deleting a bookmark

Here's how	Here's why
1 Open the Bookmark dialog box	In the Links group, click Bookmark.
2 In the list box under Bookmark name, select **cancer**	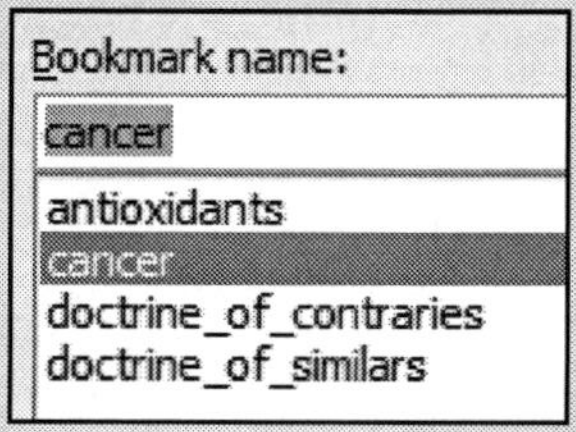
Click **Delete**	The bookmark name is deleted from the list. You aren't prompted to confirm the deletion.
3 Close the Bookmark dialog box	
4 Update the document	

Creating cross-references

Explanation

A *cross-reference* is text that refers to an item somewhere else in a document. For example, a typical cross-reference might use the following structure: "Refer to Figure 1." You can create cross-references to numbered items, headings, bookmarks, footnotes, endnotes, equations, figures, or tables. In Word, you can press Ctrl and click a cross-reference to navigate directly to the referenced item.

To create a cross-reference to a figure:

1. Place the insertion point where you want to add the cross-reference, and enter any text, such as "as shown in" or "(see)."
2. Click the Insert tab.
3. In the Links group, click Cross-reference to open the Cross-reference dialog box, shown in Exhibit 6-24.
4. From the Reference type list, select the type of item you're referring to (such as Figure, in this example).
5. In the "For which caption" list, select the figure for which you want to add a cross-reference.
6. Click Insert to insert the cross-reference.
7. Click Close.

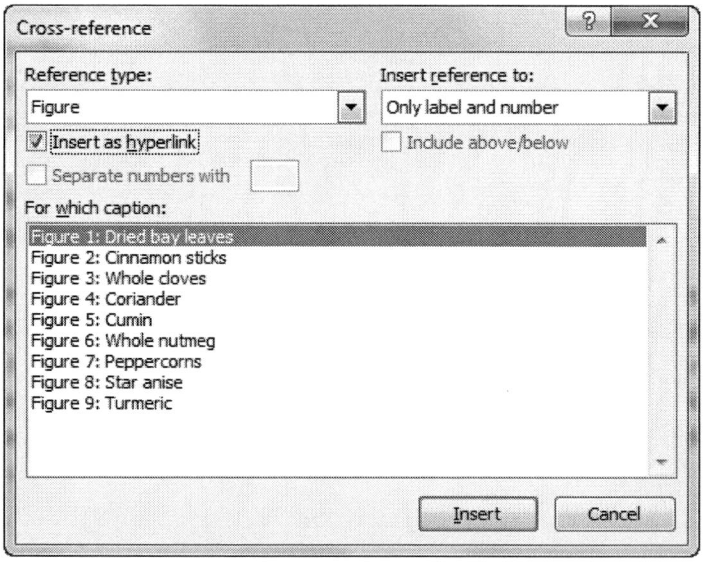

Exhibit 6-24: The Cross-reference dialog box

Updating a cross-reference

After you add a cross-reference to a figure, the figure's number might change. For example, if you add or remove a figure, the cross-referenced figure's number might change. If that happens, you'll have to update the cross-reference to reflect the figure's new number. To update a cross-reference, right-click it and choose Update Field.

Do it!

D-4: Creating a cross-reference

Here's how	Here's why
1 Scroll to view the first Spice descriptions page, which includes the figure and text for bay leaves	(This is page 3.) You'll add a cross-reference to the figure of the bay leaves.
2 In the first paragraph's last sentence, place the insertion point after "whole"	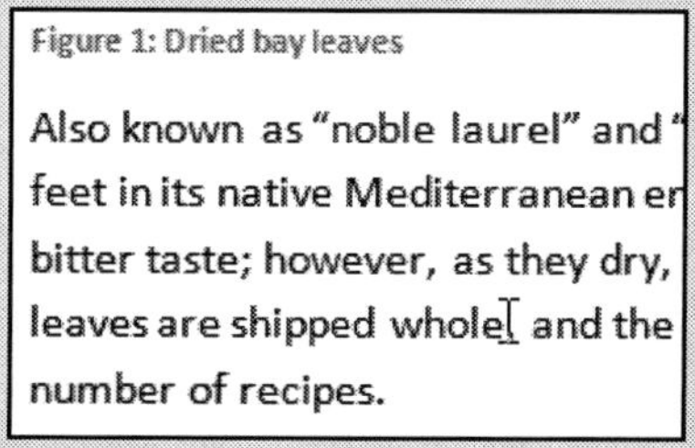 The insertion point should be between "whole" and the comma.
Type **, as shown in**	
Press SPACEBAR	
3 Click the **Insert** tab	(If necessary.) You'll insert the cross-reference to the figure.
4 In the Links group, click **Cross-reference**	 To open the Cross-reference dialog box.
From the Reference type list, select **Figure**	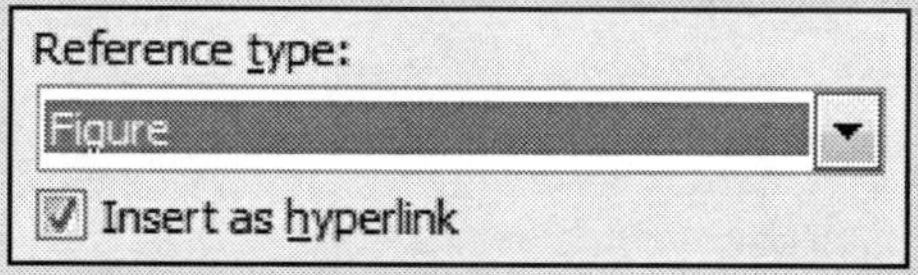 By default, "Insert as hyperlink" is checked, so you'll be able to press Ctrl and click the cross-reference to navigate to the figure.
5 From the "Insert reference to" list, select **Only label and number**	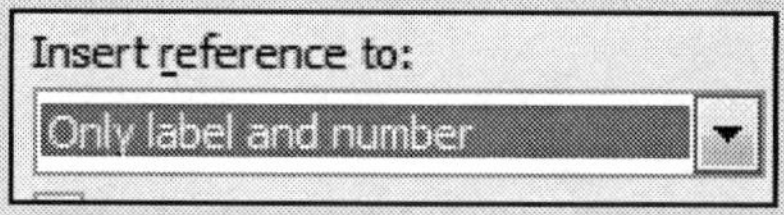 To specify that only the word "Figure" and the figure number will be included in the cross-reference. The rest of the figure's caption won't be included.
Under "For which caption," verify that **Figure 1: Dried bay leaves** is selected	
Click **Insert**	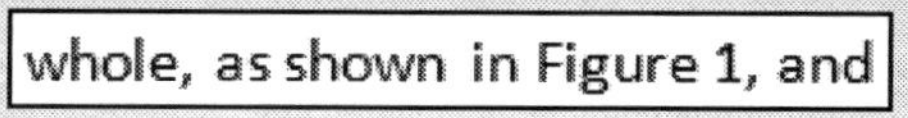 To insert the cross-reference.

6 Click **Close**	To close the Cross-reference dialog box.
7 Press CTRL and click **Figure 1**	(Click the cross-reference you just inserted.) To navigate to the figure itself.
8 Update and close the document	

Topic E: Web frames

Explanation

Web frames can be used to create a Web-site header that remains at the top of the screen while the reader browses a site, or to create a table of contents that stays on the screen while readers go to different pages in a Web site. When you use frames, a Web page is divided into sections, and each section is a frame. The container that holds a group of frames is called a *frames page*. In Word, you can create and modify frames pages.

Creating frames pages

You can save a Word document as a Web page. If it's a large document, you might want to create a frames page to divide the Web page into several frames, as shown in Exhibit 6-25. You can then use these frames to display different types of content, such as the table of contents or the information in the document.

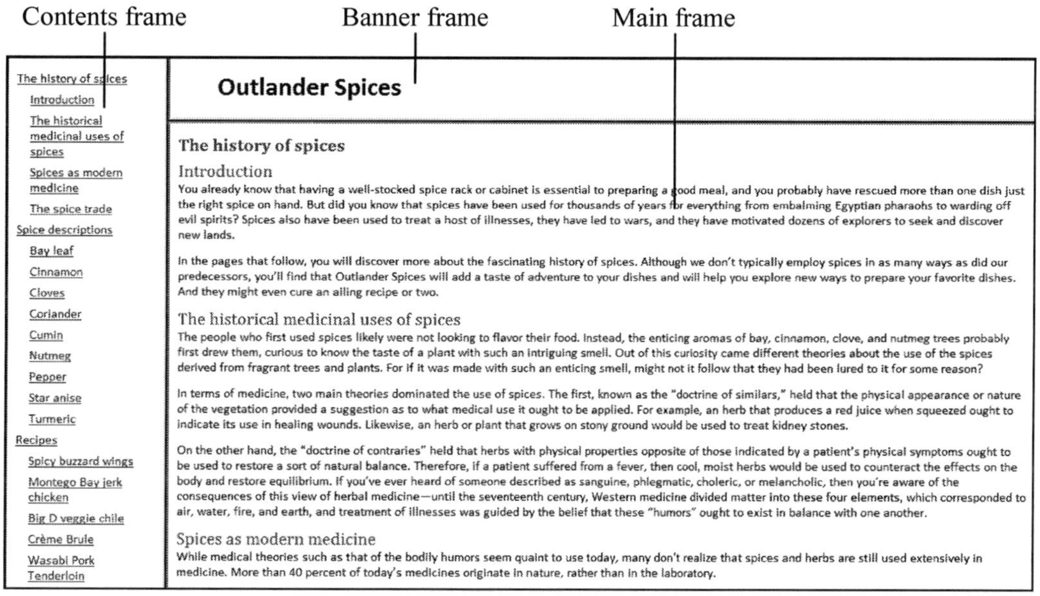

Exhibit 6-25: A frames page

To create a frames page from a document:

1. Open the document.
2. Add the necessary frames buttons to the Quick Access toolbar. You might add buttons such as Frame Properties, New Frame Above, New Frame Below, New Frames Page, and Table of Contents in Frame.
3. On the Quick Access toolbar, click the New Frames Page button to add frames to display the document content.
4. Click the Table of Contents in Frame button to create the table of contents in a separate frame.
5. Save the frames page as a Web page.

Do it!

E-1: Creating a frames page

The files for this activity are in Student Data folder **Unit 6\Topic E**.

Here's how	Here's why
1 Open Frames	
2 Customize the Quick Access toolbar to include these buttons: **Frame Properties** **New Frame Above** **New Frames Page** **Table of Contents in Frame**	On the Quick Access toolbar, click the Customize Quick Access Toolbar button and choose More Commands to open the Word Options dialog box. Verify that Quick Access Toolbar is selected in the left pane. From the "Choose commands from" list, select All commands. In the list of commands, select each command, and click Add. Click OK.
3 On the Quick Access toolbar, click 	(The New Frames Page button.) A frames page opens with the contents of the Frames document.
4 Click 	(The Table of Contents in Frame button.) The frames page is divided into two frames. The first frame displays the table of contents. The second frame displays the information in the document.
5 Click the **File** tab and click **Save As**	To open the Save As dialog box.
Edit the File name box to read **My frames**	
From the Save as type list, select **Web Page**	You'll save the frames page as a Web page with the .htm extension. Save it in Student Data folder Unit 6\Topic E.
Click **Save**	
6 Place the insertion point as shown	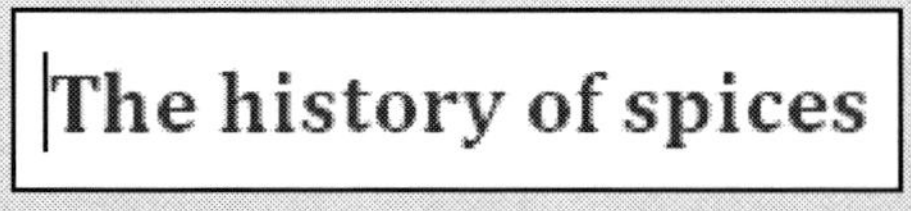 To select the main frame.
Click 	(The New Frame Above button is on the Quick Access toolbar.) A new frame appears above the right frame.
7 Enter **Outlander Spices**	To specify a heading in the top frame.
Format the text as bold 24 pt	
Deselect the text	
8 Update the file	

9	Start Windows Explorer	Click Start and choose All Programs, Accessories, Windows Explorer.
	Browse to the current topic folder	You'll open My frames.htm in a Web browser.
10	Double-click **My frames**	(Maximize the browser window, if necessary.) The table of contents appears in the left frame, "Outlander Spices" appears in the upper-right frame, and the main document text appears in the lower-right frame.
11	In the Table of Contents frame, click **Cinnamon**	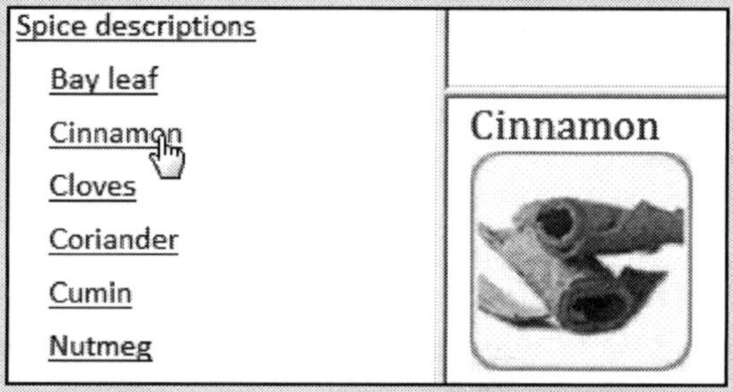 The lower-right frame displays the content describing cinnamon. When you click any heading in the Table of Contents frame, the corresponding content appears in the lower-right frame.
12	Switch to Word	

Modifying frames

Explanation

You can modify a frame by using the Frame Properties dialog box. You can change frame properties such as width, height, and border color. You can also specify when you want the scrollbars to appear in frames. To do so, click the Borders tab and select an option from the "Show scrollbars in browser" list. If the "Frame is resizable in browser" option is cleared, the frames cannot be resized.

To modify a frame:

1. In the frames page, select the frame you want to modify.
2. On the Quick Access toolbar, click Frame Properties to open the Frame Properties dialog box.
3. Specify the changes. You can use the Frame tab to change the frame's properties, such as its width and color. You can use the Borders tab to modify the borders, as shown in Exhibit 6-26.
4. Click OK.

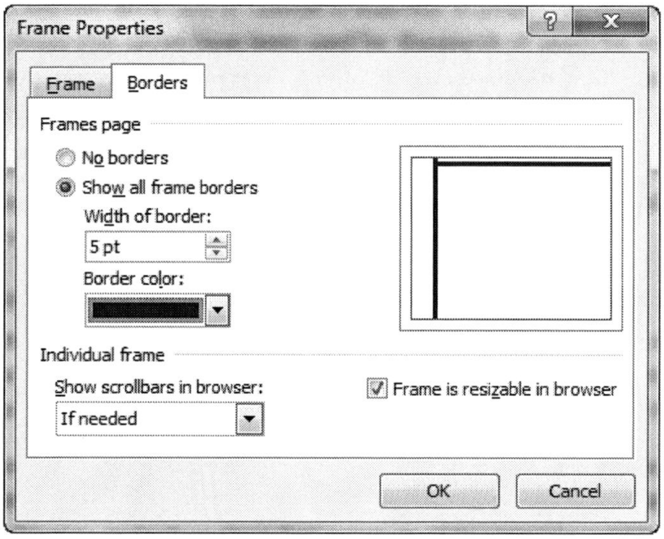

Exhibit 6-26: The Borders tab in the Frame Properties dialog box

Do it!

E-2: Modifying frames

Here's how	Here's why
1 Resize the top-right frame, as shown	 To decrease the size of the top frame.
2 Place the insertion point in the left frame, as shown	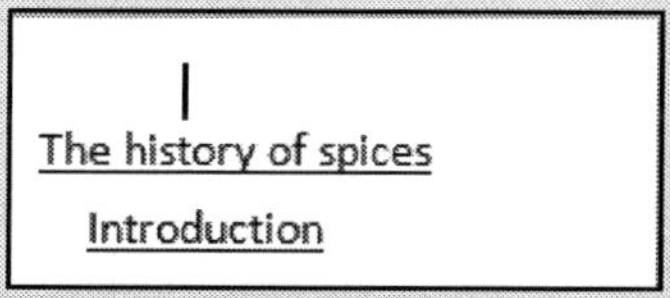 You'll change the size of this frame.
3 Click 	(The Frame Properties button is on the Quick Access toolbar.) To open the Frame Properties dialog box.
Under Size, in the Width box, enter **2**	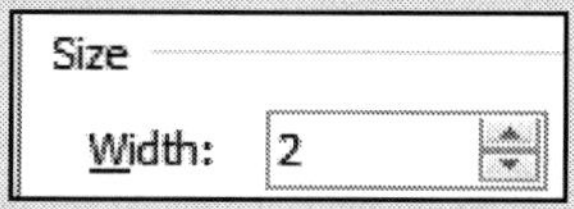 To specify the size of the frame as 2 inches.
Click **OK**	The left frame's width decreases.
4 Open the Frame Properties dialog box	(Click the Frame Properties button.) You'll customize all of the frame borders.
Click the **Borders** tab	
5 In the Width of border box, enter **5 pt**	To change the size of the borders.
From the Border color list, select **Blue**	To change the frame borders to blue. Your Frame Properties dialog box should match Exhibit 6-26.
Click **OK**	The borders are now thicker and blue.
6 Update the file	
7 Switch to Internet Explorer	
Refresh the view	(Click the Refresh button on the toolbar, press F5, or choose View, Refresh.) To display the modified frames.
8 Close Internet Explorer	
9 Update and close the document	

Unit summary: Long documents

Topic A In this topic, you created a **master document** by inserting subdocuments. You also deleted subdocuments. In addition, you created a cover page.

Topic B In this topic, you learned how to create, modify, and update a **table of contents**. You also inserted figure **captions**. You then created, modified, and updated a table of figures.

Topic C In this topic, you created **index** entries and subentries by using the Mark Index Entry dialog box. You also created, modified, and updated a **bibliography** and a **table of authorities**. Finally, you inserted, edited, and deleted a **footnote**.

Topic D In this topic, you created and worked with **bookmarks** by using the Bookmark dialog box. You also created **cross-references**.

Topic E In this topic, you created a Web page and divided it into **frames**. You also added a table of contents in a frame and modified the frame properties.

Independent practice activity

In this activity, you'll create a table of contents, add a caption, and mark several words as index entries.

The files for this activity are in Student Data folder **Unit 6\Unit summary**.

1 Open Practice and save it as **My practice**.

2 Create a table of contents at the beginning of the document. Show only two levels and use the Formal format. Compare your screen to Exhibit 6-27.

3 On page 4, for the image of the chicken dish, add a caption that reads **Figure 1: Spiced chicken**.

4 On page 3, after the bullet items, mark **Southwestern** as a main index entry. In the same paragraph, add **Asian** as a main index entry. On the next page, in the first paragraph, mark **cookbook** and **recipes** as main index entries.

5 At the end of the document, insert a page break. On the new blank page, generate a two-column index in the Modern format, as shown in Exhibit 6-28.

6 Update and close the document.

Exhibit 6-27: The table of contents after Step 2

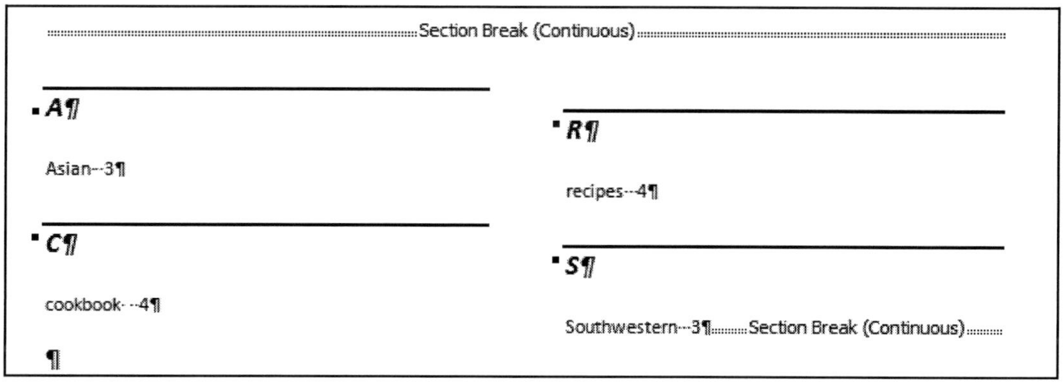

Exhibit 6-28: The generated index after Step 5

Review questions

1 Which tab contains the tools for adding subdocuments to a master document?

A Home

B Developer

C Page Layout

D Outlining

2 How is Master Document view different from Outline view?

3 By default, what determines the text that is included in a table of contents?

A Heading styles

B Bookmarks

C Index entries

D Cross-references

4 How can you add a caption to a Word figure or table?

5 How can you create a table of figures?

6 How are endnotes different from footnotes?

7 What step must be done before you can generate an index?

A Create an outline.

B Mark the index entries.

C Switch to Print Layout view.

D Display nonprinting symbols.

8 What are the two types of index entries?

9 Which of these is a valid name for a bookmark?

A Bookmark One

B Bookmark 1

C bookmark_1

D 1_bookmark

10 If you want to divide a Web document into sections that display specific content, which button should you use?

A New Frames Page

B Chart

C IGX Graphic

D Macros

Unit 7
XML features

Unit time: 20 minutes

Complete this unit, and you'll know how to:

A Create an XML document, attach an XML schema, use XML options, and apply a transform.

Topic A: Working with XML

Explanation

Hypertext Markup Language (HTML) is a language used to construct Web pages. HTML consists of predefined tags. A *tag* is a code that specifies how a Web page should be structured or formatted. For example, the Title tag specifies a title for the Web page.

Extensible Markup Language (XML) is a standard markup language that designers use to define their own tags, something that's not possible in HTML. (HTML and XML are both offshoots of SGML: Structured Generalized Markup Language.)

XML tags

The XML tags you define will organize document content hierarchically, but the tags won't directly specify how the content should be formatted. You can create an XML tag for each item in a document that you want to isolate for formatting purposes, as shown in Exhibit 7-1. You can then output the tagged XML content to an unlimited number of formats. For example, you could create a set of XML tags that you apply to your company newsletter content. You could then output the XML content with one layout for print purposes, and with a completely different layout for Web use. Both documents would be generated from the same initial XML file.

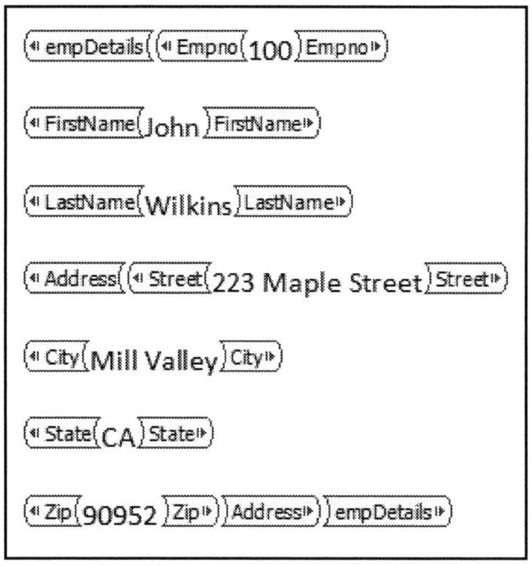

Exhibit 7-1: An XML document with tags

Attaching an XML schema

The set of XML tags you create to hierarchically structure specific content is called a *schema*. After you've applied the tags from a schema to specific content and saved it as an XML file, you can open the XML file in Word or in other applications where formatting can be specified for each XML tag. The schema used in XML is known as the *XML Schema Definition* (XSD), which is a way to describe and validate data in an XML environment. Exhibit 7-2 shows an example of an XSD file.

```
<xsd:schema xmlns:xsd="http://www.w3.org/2001/XMLSchema">

        <xsd:annotation>
         <xsd:documentation xml:lang="en">
           Employee Details schema for Outlander Spices.com
         </xsd:documentation>
        </xsd:annotation>

        <xsd:element name="empDetails" type="Empdetails"/>
        <xsd:complexType name="Empdetails">
         <xsd:sequence>
                <xsd:element name="Empno" type="xsd:int"/>
                <xsd:element name="FirstName" type="xsd:string"/>
                <xsd:element name="LastName" type="xsd:string"/>
                <xsd:element name="Address" type="USAddress"/>
         </xsd:sequence>
        </xsd:complexType>

        <xsd:complexType name="USAddress">
         <xsd:sequence>
                <xsd:element name="Street" type="xsd:string"/>
                <xsd:element name="City" type="xsd:string"/>
                <xsd:element name="State" type="xsd:string"/>
                <xsd:element name="Zip" type="xsd:decimal"/>
         </xsd:sequence>
        </xsd:complexType>
</xsd:schema>
```

Exhibit 7-2: A sample XSD

You can use Word to create an XML document based on a schema. First, you have to attach a schema to the Word document. To do so:

1. Create a document.
2. On the Developer tab, in the XML group, click Structure to open the XML Structure pane.
3. Click Templates and Add-Ins to open the Templates and Add-ins dialog box, shown in Exhibit 7-3.
4. Click Add Schema to open the Add Schema dialog box.
5. Select the desired schema and click Open. The Schema Settings dialog box appears.
6. In the URI box, enter a name for the schema. (A URI is a *Uniform Resource Identifier*—any type of name or address that refers to something on the Web.)
7. Click OK twice to close the Schema Settings dialog box and the Templates and Add-ins dialog box.

After attaching the schema, you can apply the necessary tags to the document content and save the file as an XML document. You apply a tag by selecting it from the "Choose an element to apply to your current selection" list in the XML Structure pane.

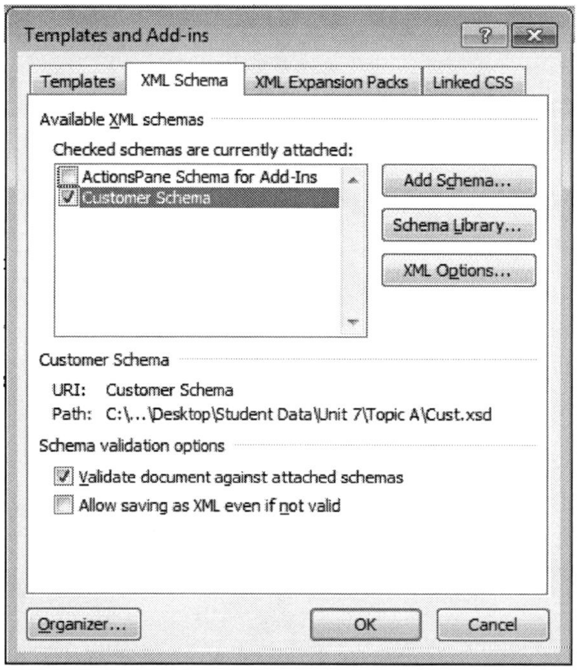

Exhibit 7-3: The XML Schema tab in the Templates and Add-ins dialog box

You can also delete an attached schema if you don't need it. To do this:

1. Open an XML document with an underlying schema.
2. Open the Templates and Add-ins dialog box.
3. Click Schema Library to open the Schema Library dialog box.
4. Select the schema you want to delete.
5. Click Delete Schema and then click Yes when prompted.
6. Click OK to return to the Templates and Add-ins dialog box; then click OK to close it.

Do it!

A-1: Attaching an XML schema to a Word document

The files for this activity are in Student Data folder **Unit 7\Topic A**.

Here's how	Here's why
1 Create a blank document	
Type the text shown	
2 Display the Developer tab	(If necessary.) Use the Word Options dialog box.
Click the **Developer** tab	
In the XML group, click **Schema**	To open the Templates and Add-ins dialog box. The XML Schema tab is active. No schemas are attached to the document.
3 Click **Add Schema**	To open the Add Schema dialog box so you can attach an XML schema to this document.
Select **Cust.xsd**	From Student Data folder Unit 7\Topic A.
4 Click **Open**	The Schema Settings dialog box opens.
In the URI box, enter **Customer Schema**	 To specify a name for the schema.
Click **OK**	To close the Schema Settings dialog box. Your Templates and Add-ins dialog box should match Exhibit 7-3.
5 Click **OK**	To close the dialog box and attach the schema to the document. The XML Structure pane tells you that no XML elements have been applied to the document.

Applying XML tags

Explanation

Elements form the basic building blocks of an XML document. Each element represents a piece of data and is typically identified by a pair of tags: a start tag and an end tag. All XML documents have a top-level parent element, called the *root element*. All other elements are nested inside the root element.

After you've attached a schema to a document, you can apply tags to the document content to specify each element. To apply XML tags:

1. Select the content that you want to tag as a given element.
2. In the pane, under "Choose an element to apply to your current selection," click the element you want to apply. The list will display only those elements that are allowed to be added at the current location.
3. Click the File tab and click Save As to open the Save As dialog box.
4. From the Save as type list, select Word XML Document.

Do it!

A-2: Applying XML tags to content

	Here's how	Here's why
1	Select the entire document	Press Ctrl+A.
	In the XML Structure pane, select **Customer {Customer schema}**	You are asked if you want to apply the Customer element to the entire document.
	Click **Apply to Entire Document**	The Customer tag is applied to the entire document.
	Press END	To deselect the text.
2	In the pane, verify that **Show XML tags in the document** is checked	
3	Select **1001**	
	In the XML Structure pane, select **Idno**	To apply the Idno tag to 1001.
	Apply the **CustomerName** tag to **Western Spice Retailers**	Select Western Spice Retailers in the document, and then select CustomerName in the XML Structure pane.
4	Select the four address lines	
	In the pane, select **Address**	To apply the Address tag to the entire selection.
5	Select **120 Summit Ave**	You'll group the text under the Address tag.
6	In the pane, select **Street**	To apply the Street tag to the selection.

7 Select **San Francisco**

In the pane, select **City** — To apply the City tag to the selection.

8 Apply the **State** tag to **CA**

Apply the **Zip** tag to **94138**

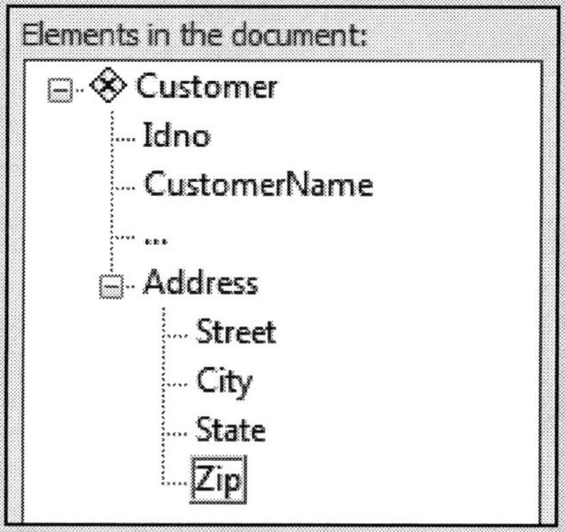

The XML Structure pane displays the elements that you've added to the document.

9 Save the document as an XML document with the name **My customer**

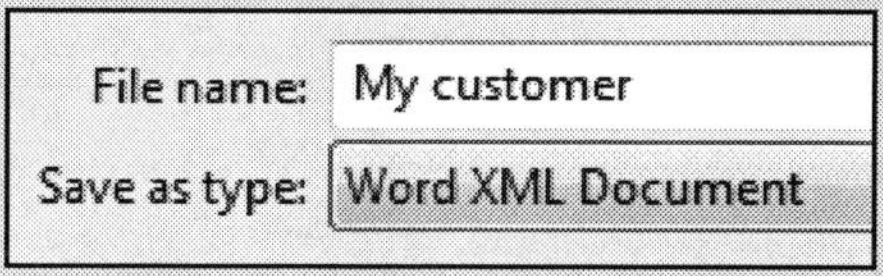

In the Save As dialog box, be sure to select Word XML Document from the Save as type list.

Using the XML Options dialog box

Explanation

As you create an XML document with an underlying XML schema, Word checks for schema violations. If violations are found, Word displays an error message stating that a schema violation has occurred and the document cannot be created. Therefore, you need to apply all of the tags in the underlying schema to the document before it can be created.

You can control the schema validation options in the XML Options dialog box. Use the XML view options to show advanced error messages, to hide alias names, and to show placeholder text for empty elements.

To modify the XML options:

1. In the XML Structure pane, click XML Options to open the XML Options dialog box, shown in Exhibit 7-4.
2. Under “Schema validation options,” specify how much control the schema will have on the document.
3. Under “XML view options,” check “Show advanced XML error messages” to see detailed messages.
4. Click OK.

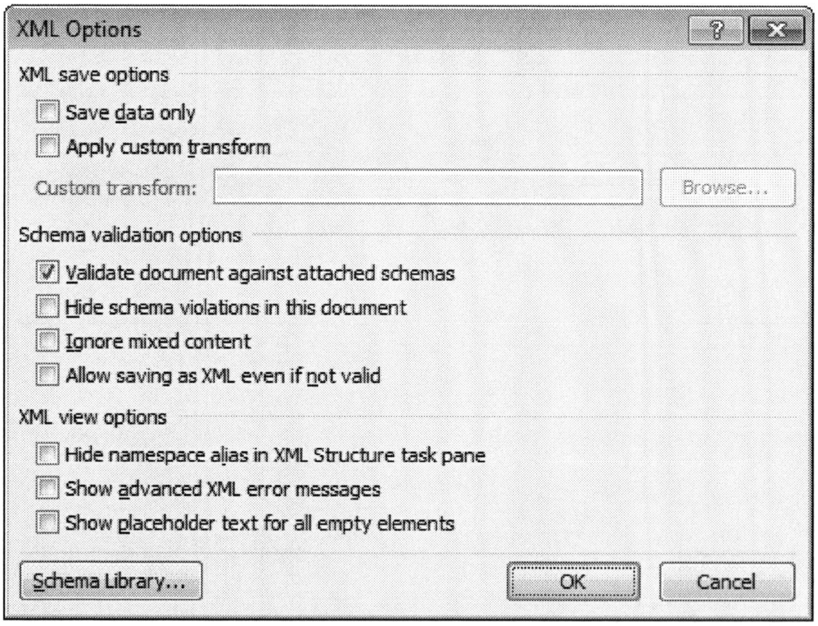

Exhibit 7-4: The XML Options dialog box

Do it!

A-3: Modifying XML options

Here's how	Here's why
1 In the XML Structure pane, click **XML Options**	(Located at the bottom of the pane.) To open the XML Options dialog box, shown in Exhibit 7-4.
2 Observe the Schema validation options	The "Validate document against attached schemas" setting tells Word to validate the document with the underlying schema before creating the XML document.
3 Under "XML view options," check **Show advanced XML error messages**	To display more-detailed messages when validation problems occur.
Click **OK**	To close the XML Options dialog box and save your changes.

Error messages

Explanation

If your document does not specify content for each tag in the schema, a schema violation occurs. Word uses several indicators to alert you to schema violations, as shown in Exhibit 7-5.

- One indication is a wavy purple line that appears to the left of the document element in which the violation occurs.
- Another indication appears in the XML Structure pane. In the “Elements in the document” list, a question-mark icon appears next to the element in which the violation occurs.

When a schema violation indicator appears, you can examine the indicated element and fix it. When you point to the question-mark icon in the XML Structure pane, a message appears, describing the violation. When you fix the violation, the schema violation indicators disappear.

Exhibit 7-5: Indicators of schema validation problems

Do it!

A-4: Testing the schema validation

Here's how	Here's why
1 In the document, select the ZIP code, including the XML tags	
Press DELETE	To delete the tag along with the data. The purple wavy line indicates that there is a schema problem.
2 In the XML Structure pane, point as shown	 The error message tells you that the Address element is incomplete. More specifically, it tells you that Zip was expected.
3 In the document, enter **94138**	To enter the ZIP code in the document.
Select **94138** and apply the **Zip** tag	In the XML Structure pane, Address no longer has the yellow question-mark icon next to it. The purple wavy line has also disappeared.
4 Update the document	
Close the XML Structure pane	
Close the document	

Applying transforms

Explanation

By default, when you create an XML document and display it in a Web browser, the document appears without any formatting, as shown in Exhibit 7-6. The formatting in an XML document is controlled by a transform and a style sheet. A *transform* is a set of presentation rules that is contained in a style sheet. A *style sheet* is a file that defines the layout of a document, such as background color or fonts.

The language commonly used for constructing a style sheet in an XML environment is called *Extensible Style Language* (XSL). A transform created by using this style sheet is known as an *Extensible Style Language Transformation* (XSLT). These files have an .xsl extension.

```
  <?xml version="1.0" encoding="UTF-8" standalone="no" ?>
- <empDetails>
    <Empno>100</Empno>
    <FirstName>John Wilkins</FirstName>
  - <Address>
      <Street>223 Maple Street</Street>
      <City>Mill Valley</City>
      <State>CA</State>
      <Zip>90952</Zip>
    </Address>
  </empDetails>
```

Exhibit 7-6: An XML document without any transforms

When you apply an XSLT to an XML document, the results of the transform appear, as shown in Exhibit 7-7. When you apply a transform, Word will ignore any data that the XSLT file doesn't use. You can apply multiple transforms to a single XML document to generate multiple versions of the file, each with a different appearance.

To apply a transform to an XML document:

1 Create an XML document.

2 Open the XML Structure pane.

3 Attach an XML schema to the document.

4 Click XML Options to open the XML Options dialog box.

5 Check "Apply custom transform."

6 Next to Custom transform, click Browse. Select the relevant XSLT and click OK.

7 Click OK to close the XML Options dialog box.

8 Save the document.

100
John Wilkins
223 Maple Street
Mill Valley
CA
90952

Exhibit 7-7: An XML document after a transform has been applied

Do it!

A-5: Discussing transforms and style sheets

Questions and answers

1 What is a transform?

2 What is a style sheet?

3 True or false? XSL is a form of style sheet.

4 What is an XSLT?

5 How can you apply a transform in Word?

Unit summary: XML features

Topic A

In this topic, you created an **XML** document by attaching an XML **schema** to a Word document and adding XML **tags** to the document content. In addition, you learned how to use the XML Options dialog box to view error messages. You also discussed how to apply **transforms**.

Independent practice activity

In this activity, you'll create an XML file, attach a schema, and specify the document elements.

The files for this activity are in Student Data folder **Unit 7\Unit summary**.

1 Create a document with the information shown in Exhibit 7-8.

2 Attach the schema Emp.xsd to this document, and specify the URI name as **Employee schema**.

3 Apply the empDetails, Empno, FirstName, LastName, Address, Street, City, State, and Zip tags, as shown in Exhibit 7-9. Fix any schema problems that occur.

4 Save the document as **My practice.xml** in the XML format. Then close the document.

5 Close Microsoft Word.

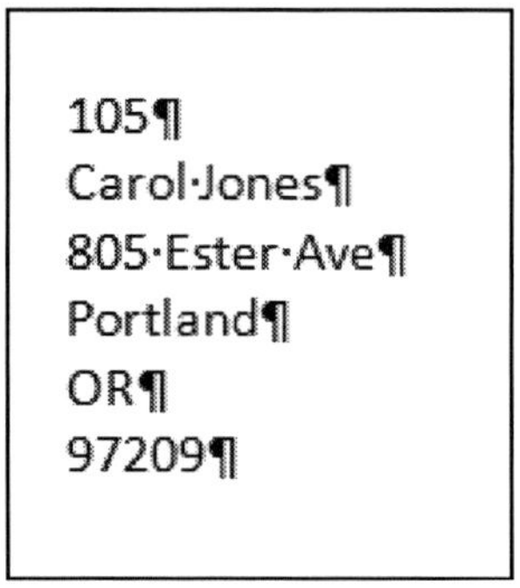

Exhibit 7-8: The data for Step 1

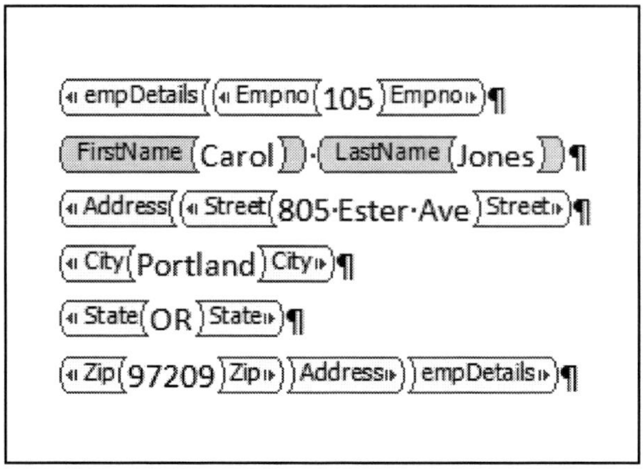

Exhibit 7-9: The tags to be attached in Step 3

Review questions

1 Which markup language is used to control the structure and format of a Web page?

A HTML

B XML

C XSD

D XSLT

2 Which markup language is used by designers to define their own tags?

A HTML

B XML

C XSD

D XSLT

3 What is a schema?

4 How do you attach a schema to a Word document?

5 As Word checks for schema violations, what happens in the document when a violation is found?

6 What is a transform?

Course summary

This summary contains information to help you bring the course to a successful conclusion. Using this information, you will be able to:

A Use the summary text to reinforce what you've learned in class.

B Determine the next courses in this series (if any), as well as any other resources that might help you continue to learn about Microsoft Word 2010.

Topic A: Course summary

Use the following summary text to reinforce what you've learned in class.

Unit summaries

Unit 1

In this unit, you learned how to specify a starting document, specify a recipient list, and add merge fields to create a **form letter**. You also learned how to **sort** and **filter** records in a recipient list. You then learned how to prepare **mailing labels**, merge a recipient list with mailing-label and envelope documents, and preview and print labels.

Unit 2

In this unit, you created an Excel worksheet object in a Word document. You also inserted an Excel file as a **linked object**, modified the data, and inserted a chart based on Excel data. You then added **background** colors and fill effects to Word documents, inserted watermarks, and applied themes.

Unit 3

In this unit, you learned how to create and run **macros** to automate tasks. In addition, you viewed and modified macro scripts in the Microsoft Visual Basic editor.

Unit 4

In this unit, you created **forms** by adding field labels and adding and modifying content controls. In addition, you protected a form by using the Restrict Formatting and Editing task pane. You also learned how to set permissions for a user to modify specified regions of a protected form. Finally, you used the **Compatibility Checker** and the **Document Inspector** and discussed **digital signatures**.

Unit 5

In this unit, you learned how to show and hide the Ribbon and how to **customize the Ribbon** by rearranging tabs, hiding tabs and commands, removing groups, and adding tabs, groups, and commands. You then customized the **Quick Access toolbar** by adding, rearranging, and removing buttons. In addition, you assigned custom **keyboard shortcuts** to Word commands.

Unit 6

In this unit, you created a **master document** by inserting subdocuments. Next, you learned how to create a **table of contents** and a table of figures. In addition, you created an index, a bibliography, a footnote, endnotes, bookmarks, and cross-references. Finally, you divided a Web page document into **frames** and modified frame properties and contents.

Unit 7

In this unit, you created an **XML** document by attaching an XML schema to a Word document and adding XML tags to the document content. In addition, you learned how to use the XML Options dialog box to display **error messages**. Finally, you discussed how to apply **transforms**.

Topic B: Continued learning after class

It is impossible to learn how to use any software effectively in a single day. To get the most out of this class, you should begin working with Microsoft Word 2010 to perform real tasks as soon as possible. We also offer resources for continued learning.

Next courses in this series

This is the last course in this series.

Other resources

For more information, visit www.axzopress.com.

Glossary

Bookmark
An electronically marked location in a document, which you can navigate to directly by clicking the associated bookmark entry in the Bookmark dialog box.

Caption
Text that identifies a figure or table.

Class 2 digital certificate
A type of digital certificate for people who publish software individually.

Class 3 digital certificate
A type of digital certificate for companies that publish software; it guarantees the identity of the publishing company.

Content controls
Placeholders for storing data in a form. Content controls can also guide and restrict the user's actions and tell the user how to complete the form.

Cross-reference
A notation that refers to items somewhere else in a document. You can create cross-references to numbered items, headings, bookmarks, footnotes, endnotes, figures, or tables.

Data source
A repository of information that is used to populate the main document in a mail merge.

Digital certificate
An attachment that guarantees security for a document.

Digital signature
An electronic security stamp that is used to authenticate a form, macro, or document.

Drop-down list field
A type of form field used to provide a list of values from which users can select an option.

Extensible Markup Language (XML)
A markup language that enables designers to define their own tags.

Extensible Style Language (XSL)
The language commonly used for constructing style sheets in an XML environment.

Extensible Style Language Transformation (XSLT)
A transform (set of presentation rules) created by using an XSL style sheet.

Field label
Text that describes the data stored in a field.

Footnote
A note that appears at the bottom of a page, providing explanations about or references to information on that page.

Frame
An individual section of a Web page, displaying content that can typically be scrolled without scrolling the content in other sections.

Frames page
The container that holds a group of frames for a Web page.

Hypertext Markup Language (HTML)
A language used to construct Web pages. HTML consists of predefined tags, or code.

Macro
A collection of actions that are recorded and that can be played back in one step, allowing users to automate tasks.

Master document
A document containing a collection of subdocuments.

Merge fields
Mail-merge placeholders that display information from the recipient list.

PDF (Portable Document Format)
A fixed-layout file format that preserves a document's appearance and enables file sharing with people who don't have the file's source application.

Recipient list
A repository of information that is used to populate the main document in a mail merge.

Schema
The set of XML tags you create to hierarchically structure specific content.

Starting document
A mailing label, envelope, or form letter that is used in a mail merge.

Style sheet
A file that defines the layout of a document. The formatting in XML documents is controlled by transforms and style sheets.

Subdocuments
The individual documents that are inserted into a single document, which becomes the master document.

Table of authorities
A list of expert sources of information in a document and their corresponding page numbers.

Table of figures
A list of elements, such as pictures, contained in a document. The table lists each element's caption and page number.

Tag
Code that identifies content in order to control how it is formatted or structured.

Transform
A set of presentation rules that is contained in a style sheet.

URI (Uniform Resource Identifier)
Any type of name or address that refers to an object on the Web.

Watermark
Any text or image that can be seen behind the text in a document.

XPS (XML Paper Specification)
A fixed-layout file format that preserves a document's appearance and enables file sharing with people who don't have the file's source application.

XSD (XML Schema Definition)
A language used to describe and validate data in an XML environment.

Index

K

L

M

O

P

Q

R

S

T

V

W

X